Ten Came Back

Their own stories and what they can teach us about reclaiming our friends and family

Tim Lale & Pat Habada

Pacific Press® Publishing Association
Nampa, Idaho
Oshawa, Ontario, Canada

Edited by Kenneth R. Wade
Cover art by Consuelo Udave
Designed by Tim Larson

Lale, Tim, 1964-
    Ten who came back : their own stories and what
they can teach us about reclaiming our friends and
family / Tim Lale, Pat Habada.
        p.   cm.
    ISBN 0-8163-1406-3 (pbk. : alk paper)
    1. Seventh-day Adventists—Membership. 2. Ex-
church members—United States—Case studies.
3.   Seventh-day   Adventists—Interviews.
4.   Ex-church   members—United   States—
Interviews. I. Habada, Patricia A. II. Title.
BX6154.L28   1998
286.7'32—dc21   97-25908
                                          CIP

98 99 00 01 02 • 5 4 3 2 1

Dedication

Linda, Megan, Brianna, and Kathryn,
I hope and pray that you will welcome God
to walk next to you every day of your lives.

To Jo, whose book will be finished
in the kingdom.
In loving memory.

Contents

Foreword

I've never seriously left the church. I've flirted with the idea and have even been absent from church for weeks on end. I once was unfairly released from church employment through a set of circumstances that gave me every reason to say goodbye to Adventism forever. But I've never quite done it.

So why would I write a Foreword for a book about people who have left the church and then found reasons to reconnect? Much like the authors, I have interviewed dozens of former and still inactive Adventists—primarily in their thirties and forties.

I'm a boomer (the generation born between 1946 and 1964) and the majority of my generation is absent from church most weekends. I've grieved more than once while listening to stories of people who felt they had been "cut off" from their church by those in leadership.

I noticed several trends I believe you will find reflected in the stories profiled in this book.

1. When people sense grace in a church, they attend it whether or not it is the one in which they grew up. When they sense judgment, they leave, often without fanfare or protest. If you ask them why they left, they tell you it is because churched people tend to honor rules more than relationships.

2. Congregations have "reputations" among former/inactive members. Make no mistake, they talk to each other, and word gets around quickly if your church is a safe place to return for fellowship and worship.

3. Integrity of leadership is key to a returning member's willingness to consider a church. Honest, informal, fun-loving leaders win the trust of inactive members. If in those first few minutes that person does not sense these traits from the leader (pastor or other key persons), the former/inactive member becomes "out of reach" for several more years.

I would encourage you to take a long hard look at your church. Is it the kind of environment where people you haven't seen in a while would feel good about getting back together again? Are you a safe person to be around for a former/inactive Adventist? Is your congregation a safe place where absent Adventists (or persons of any faith) would feel comfortable?

If these questions trouble you, search this book carefully for clues on how to be the type of person who wins people back to fellowship and leadership. If you're looking for help, the Center for Creative Ministry can supply you with materials that will help make your church even more attractive. You can contact the Center on the Internet at www.creativeministry.org or at (800) 272-4664.

Paul Richardson, Director
Center for Creative Ministry

Introduction

Tim Lale

During the years I was absent from the Seventh-day Adventist Church, I watched a movie called *The Big Chill*. I think I watched it 15 times in a couple of years. It is the ultimate baby-boomer movie, and if you don't remember it, it's about a group of college friends who, many years after going their separate ways, gather for the funeral of one of their number who has committed suicide. The group then spends the weekend in the home of one of the guys in the group.

I am a little unnerved that even though I was born in the last year of the boomer era (1964) and don't consider myself a baby boomer, I craved the atmosphere of that movie. I exited the church during my college years, and I needed an anchor then. I yearned to be part of a small community that would give me, first, a sense of affirmation and fulfillment, and second, some philosophical answers to life's meaning. And I wanted answers in the vocabulary of my generation.

I did have a loose group of wonderful friends around me at college, but most of them were no more anchored than I was. The circle of former college buddies in *The Big Chill* (never mind that it was fictitious) came closest to my ideal.

This is what many people are looking for in a church. No matter your age, your struggles, or your doctrine, you want to find the group that will affirm you and help you get through life on this earth.

If you have been in the church and then left it, chances are you've tried to find a replacement. So why would you ever come back?

The next step

You will find in this book a response to at least some of the questions raised in the book *Ten Who Left* (Pacific Press, 1995). In this sequel, ten Seventh-day Adventists explain why they pulled away from the group we all know and then came back. Each has individual reasons, and a different theme emerges from each set of circumstances. But somehow they all came back to the group.

On the couch

I've taken a trick from *The Big Chill* to produce one of the interviews in this book. At one point in the movie, William Hurt sits on the couch in the living room with a video camera pointed at himself. He sits on the left side of the couch and asks a philosophical question that's troubling him. Then he moves to the right side and answers it.

I interviewed myself for one of the chapters in this

book in a similar way. With a tape recorder running in front of me, I asked each question on my list and then (without getting up) answered it as though I were talking to a complete stranger. I also transcribed the interview almost word for word to preserve the conversational structure. You'll have to take my word on this. You can read chapter 6 to find out whether it worked or not.

My coauthor, Pat, says . . .

Tim and I might be considered the odd couple of editing; we are so different. The obvious: he's a man; I'm a woman. He's tall, slender, blondish, and young. Me? I'm short (let's skip the shape business), grayish, and as my nephew might say, I look like a million dollars—old and green and wrinkled. Well, maybe not green, but I am a grandmother, and I've earned my gray hair. Hopefully, many of the wrinkles come from all the smiles I like to think I showered on the students who suffered through the twenty years I spent in the classrooms of Adventist schools.

Tim left the church during his college years. Me? I didn't have the desire, or maybe it was the courage. You just didn't leave the church in my day. You married a "good Adventist boy," and you settled down and raised kids—three in my case. I guess I'm a dyed-in-the-wool Adventist, about as conservative in my lifestyle as Adventists come. That's not to say I haven't had my problems with the church at times. But I've managed to come to grips with most of the things that bug me, though I certainly would like to see women ordained.

Although I'm different from Tim, we do share one very important thing: we love our God, and we love our church. And we share a grave concern for those

who have left and the many who even now are thinking about leaving. Now and then I run into former
students who have left the church, and I ask myself
why. Did I do all I could to instill in them the values
a Christian needs to survive in the world today? Could
I have done more? Even more frightening, did I do
something to turn them away?

Perhaps we will discover some of the answers as
we talk with a few of them. What were some of the
influences that led them away, and what led them
back?

Join us as we seek answers.

Chapter 1

Elizabeth

> **late fifties, divorced, school teacher**

What was your earliest experience with the Seventh-day Adventist Church?

My father's parents were longtime Adventists. My dad left the church and married my mother, and then his mother converted my mother when I was about six years old. Daddy never came back to the church, but he never gave us a hard time about it. I'm the oldest of eight, and Mother raised all of us in the church. I was baptized during the first baptism in our new church when it opened in 1953. I graduated from an Adventist academy and went for two years to an Adventist college. Then I transferred to a public university and graduated.

I played the piano in the children's division and was youth leader and did all the things you do when you're a young person active in the church.

How old were you when you got baptized?
Thirteen.

Do you think you became a converted Christian then?

I think when I look back over my life, I always knew intellectually. For most Adventists, most Christians, I think there are times of great spirituality and times of less. It ebbs and flows in your life. I would hope that people as they grow would grow further into it and back away less each time so the growth would be upward. But I don't think that's what happened to me. One of my ebbs was terribly bad.

What led you away from the church?

I married a non-Adventist, and we had two kids. We were married for thirteen years. He had his own business when we first married. I took my kids to church and Sabbath School all the time, and that was no problem with him. Then he decided to go back to college and get his degree, since I had mine. So he sold his business and started working at the bars here in the city to fit work around his school schedule.

He ended up being in charge of one of the bars. But he got his life pretty messed up while he was there. You can't avoid being drawn in. He's sorry now. It was just one of those disastrous things that happens. And by the time you realize what's going on, it's too late. He and I are very good friends now. But that didn't stop what happened.

How did you leave that situation?

The marriage ended mutually, and, of course, at the time of the divorce I found myself with two kids to raise. I had been teaching part time at the local junior academy, because I already had my degree but not my credentials. I had enjoyed my teaching so thoroughly.

I was sitting in church one day, and the pastor was preaching. This was right after my divorce. He was saying that when God calls you, He will let you know in unmistakable terms. It just hit me all of a sudden. "I want to be a teacher."

I went home to Sabbath lunch at my mother's, and my dad was there too. And I said, "I want to teach. I want to go back to school and teach. I don't know how I can afford to do this and raise my kids." And my dad loaned me the money for that graduate work.

So I got my fifth year and my credentials the next year at an Adventist graduate school. I had a tremendous experience with the Lord during that time. I taught at a junior academy for two years and then moved to a senior academy for six years. I just had a wonderful time with the kids and had a good time with the Lord.

I think what happened is, I got stressed out on my job. One year I taught nine classes in seven periods. I was student association sponsor, yearbook sponsor, senior class sponsor, and a single mother of two academy kids. I hit burnout so bad.

And another problem included unwanted attention from one of the teachers.

Someone at the school was paying attention to you?

This was a fellow teacher whose classroom was right across the hall from mine. His wife was my best friend, and his son was the same age as my kids. In fact, one of his sons was seriously dating my daughter during their junior and senior years in high school.

We went camping as families together, and there were several other families who went along. We just did stuff together all the time.

One day he showed up at my house to tell me that he was in love with me. Well, this was not acceptable. And it was really awkward because I had to work with him at school. Our kids were dating, our social paths were intertwined, and we were on a small school faculty.

I did the best I could to keep it cool and keep him at arm's length. He pursued me for a year and a half.

Was he married at the time?
Yes.

And it was resolved by your moving away?
Yes. I felt like I was walking a tightrope, trying to keep from saying to him things like, "You're an animal. Stay out of my life," which is probably what I should have said. Instead, I was saying things like, "This isn't the right thing to do. You shouldn't be over here. Don't come and see me." I went out of my way to avoid situations where we could possibly be alone together. And it was just really awkward.

So when my son graduated from academy, I took what was supposed to be a year's leave of absence and went to a public graduate school. It was my excuse for "running" from a bad situation I couldn't seem to resolve. While I was there, I took one year off completely from teaching and then I taught at a junior academy for a year, half time.

Did any of this affect the way you saw the church?
Yes, because it was one of several things that happened then. It happened about the same time I took the side of another teacher who had been fired, and I

ended up in a lot of hot water for taking his side. They admitted I was one of the best teachers they'd ever had on the staff, but they didn't like the political side I took in this, which I considered a moral stance. I caught a lot of flak from some of the community on that. You know how those things can split a community.

When I went over to graduate school, the community I had been a part of for six years just went on functioning as a community, and nobody came over to see me or visit me. I was all of a sudden a stranger. Out of sight, out of mind. It hurt.

Then at the next church I went to, a deacon there, a widower with some kids, started dating me, and we went out two or three times. He came over to my apartment one night and raped me, and I was not happy about that. And I never said anything about it. So among all those experiences, I was hurting, besides being burned out on my job.

And it all just kind of tied together.

It was during that time, after being single for ten years, that I met my second husband. When he showed up and wrapped two arms around me and said, "I love you, marry me, I'll take care of you, you're wonderful," I did. I was very vulnerable and put myself in a position of even more pain. But marrying him went against the grain of everything, every standard I had set for myself.

I was burned out and tired and then I quit looking at the Lord and looked at people around me. I said, "There's too much of this going on," and "I'm really upset with the way the General Conference is spending our money," and "I'm upset with the caliber of some of the teachers in our schools," and "I'm upset with some of the principals who are leading our schools." I was tired enough that I said to myself, "This whole bureaucracy is in trouble." And that led to the discouragement that allowed me to walk away.

How far away did you go and for how long?

About ten years. Actually, I didn't really walk away from the church. When I got married again, I expected to continue attending church. I didn't realize I was marrying an abuser. He moved me away from my family to a place where there was no church. If you know anything about emotional abuse, you know that isolation is one of the keys. He isolated me from my church family and my regular family. And it was just easier for me, trying to appease him, to let go of these things, trying to make him let up on the abuse.

And then I got out of the habit of going to church. Finally we moved to the next state, and there were some churches close by. I was in so much pain by then I didn't think there was any answer to pain. And I thought the commitment I had made to the marriage was something I needed to see through and see if I could work it out.

We lived there for two years, and I had the opportunity to go to church but didn't. Even the doctor I went to there was an Adventist, but he didn't know I was. I never even talked about it with him.

So you thought you couldn't be part of the church.

I couldn't be part of the church if I wanted to make my marriage work. And I felt torn between the two. I had made this commitment to the marriage, and it was more unpleasant to go with the church than it was unpleasant to go with the marriage, because the church didn't get all over my case when I went with marriage, but the husband got all over my case when

I went with the church.

I don't know if you've had any dealings with women who have been emotionally and verbally abused (in fact, my situation had reached the point where it was starting to turn physical), but the abuse denies your perception of reality. The abuser calls you vicious names, denies you any kind of confirmation, and withholds affection as a way of manipulating you. He or she isolates you from your support group so you don't have anyone to turn to for a reality check. And pretty soon you don't know what's right and what's wrong, and you think you're at fault for all the things that seem to be wrong.

I thought I was alone in experiencing this. And I thought I was doing something wrong. I thought that if I could just work harder, give more, do it better, look better, be better, that I could fix everything.

But I was digging myself into a pit, because the more I did, the fewer compliments I got. It reached a point where there was never a Please, never a Thank you, never an I love you, but filthy words. I mean, my father may not have been an Adventist when I was growing up, but he never swore at the kids. He never raised his voice. And here's my husband swearing at me in language I'd never heard in my life and calling me names and intimidating me with the sound of his voice and his anger. You can get pretty helpless in those kinds of situations. You get to the point where you're so full of fear you'd rather do anything than bring on one of those attacks. So it was less painful for me to stay away from the church.

When did you first think of returning? What prompted it?

We moved to yet another state. I had seen when we came into the little town we lived in that there

was a sign that said "Seventh-day Adventist Church."
And I thought to myself, *I don't care what my husband says, I'm going to church.*

We were running a dairy, and I was working seven
days a week in the dairy, milking morning and night.
For a year I just never got to church. By then I wasn't
keeping Sabbath or anything. Just trying to keep the
marriage together and keep myself sane. I'd quit talking to God and was just numb from one end of me to
the other.

A year ago, my baby sister died. She had Down's
syndrome and was diabetic, and she died of complications of diabetes. I planned to go home for the funeral even though it made my husband very angry.

Well, I came home, and, of course, I knew people in
the church, because I had never really lost touch with
that home church. Every time I visited my mother, I
went to church with her. And a lot of the old members were still there, and the pastor there now had
been the pastor of a church I attended while I was
teaching junior academy and going to graduate school.

So the connections—well, you know how small the
Adventist world is.

Everybody was really glad to see me, but there was
this sense of facing myself at the time of the funeral,
and the pain of losing my sister. And I thought, *I've
been gone too long.* And I started taking little tiny
baby steps, but they were so tiny.

I went back to my husband, and I went to church
in the small town where I lived. I walked into the
church, and I sat down in the very back row. I deliberately came late, and I was going to sneak out during the closing song so nobody could catch me or say
anything to me or get acquainted with me. I was going to hide, but I wanted to go. I felt like I needed to

reach out to God, and that was where to begin.

They didn't let me get away with that. They reached out and wrapped their arms around me and absolutely loved me. They called me on the phone, they caught me downtown, they hugged me when I walked into church. It was absolutely incredible, the love I got from those people. And that was what pulled me back and gave me the strength to leave my marriage and make my commitment to God.

People say, "Oh, you left your marriage." Well, yes, I did. And with all the people who were praying about it, God told me to go. I mean, in a voice that was as verbal as I can hear your voice.

So you were going through a process of praying about it for a long time?

Yes, for a long time. My sister, whose husband is a conference treasurer, had her prayer group praying for me, and my mother had a group at home praying for me, and a group at the little church in our town started praying for me.

I thought, *If they can love me like this, maybe God can love what's left of me*. And He did, and He does. It's just incredible being with Him again.

How long did it take for you to decide which way to go?

My sister died in August. I left my husband in March. But I knew before I left that I was going to. And it only took about three months of their loving me right back into the church. The minister there tracked down my membership, which was still at the last church I had gone to, and found out it was still valid.

When I started going back, I paid pretty bitterly.

My husband told me he didn't want those blankety-blank people in the house, they weren't his friends, and they couldn't come into the house. One of the ladies from the church came over on Valentine's Day and brought homemade rolls and bread, and I went and met her outside because I was afraid of what my husband would say to her if she came into the house. He didn't hesitate to eat the food; he thought the food was just fine.

So you can see why I was so open to being loved, why that was the key.

Later the church members asked me if I would substitute, as Sabbath School superintendent, for one of the ladies who got sick.

One of the men came up to me and said, "You have a college education." I mean, this was a little church. There were twenty members who came to church every week. I said, "Yes, I have a college degree." And he said, "We need somebody to give the sermon Sabbath." I mean, I nearly swallowed my tongue. But I went ahead and had the sermon.

These people have the most incredible church. It's growing. They told me that last Sabbath there were fifty people in attendance. And they were just jubilant. The church is the very center of their lives. They have potluck every week after church. And they study the Sabbath School lesson after the potluck in further depth. They have seasons of prayer and prayer lists they all keep. It's just an incredible thing.

And then after I left my husband and came back here to the city, I walked into my home church. One of the ladies I'd known since the fifties saw me from clear at the other end of the church, and she said, "Elizabeth!" and she came running down the hallway and wrapped both arms around me and said, "I'm so

glad to see you home. I have been praying for you."
So I ended up with the same love here, and it's been
so great.

For somebody who came out of a marriage as bar-
ren as mine, it's been an absolutely incredible experience.

And it was amazing, when I came back to the
church, my vocabulary cleaned up in about two weeks.
It was just an amazing transformation.

So there were elements of secular lifestyle that you absorbed?

Oh yes. My husband was an alcoholic as well as
being abusive. I started drinking with him. Not to
the extent that he did, but I did some. And in order to
protect myself sometimes, my vocabulary got as bad
as his in my trying to make him hear me. And I wasn't
keeping the Sabbath.

And those elements alone, the vocabulary and not
keeping the Sabbath, are two very devastating things
in terms of commandment keeping.

Some standards never went. I never lost my honesty. A few things like that.

Did the church contribute much to your formative years?

Oh yes. Because the friends I ran with in high
school were all Adventists and the people I knew. The
fun things we did were so innocent and so full of fun
that in a lot of ways I was very innocent. Not in a bad
way either. If you could keep that kind of innocence
all your life, it would be wonderful. But I just assumed
I could take people at face value and that good things
happened to good people.

I graduated from college in the early sixties, when

we didn't have the drugs and alcohol and fighting. It was still kind of an age of innocence. So when reality hit, I probably wasn't very prepared for some of it.

During the difficult times, how did you think about God? Were you just trying not to think about Him?

I just shut Him out. I knew He was there. I knew prayers were answered because I had seen prayers answered. I had had miracles in my life. I had had a living relationship with the Lord. I knew all these things, but I shut them out. How many times can you pray "Don't let my husband yell at me again" and have him come in screaming at you before you quit praying?

It's like you're in a dark tunnel and you can't claw your way out.

But I never blamed God for any of those things. My idea of Him was that sin is in this world and He can't always step in and stop it all.

It's like my uncle explained it to me one time. There are war rules, and God is operating under war rules with Satan. It's our prayers that give Him permission to intercede. But it's a battle between good and evil angels, and the good doesn't always win out. It will ultimately. Sometimes people with impure aspects in their lives can really muddy the waters in areas where things should be different.

What have you learned from the way your life has unfolded?

I don't think God gives us these bad times. I don't think it would have been His choice for me to marry my husband or for me to have been through the rape experience. I don't think God chose those things for me. But I think He is now using those experiences.

I find I'm more sensitive to other people, more accepting of the fact that maybe they're having a hard time, and what I may once have judged them over is not mine to judge. They may be having some hard times, and what they need is someone to love them and listen to them and reach out to them and pray for them. So I have a very different attitude than I did before.

Do you think of yourself as a different kind of church member than you used to be?
Yes, I have boundaries I've never had before. So I can say, "Yes, I will do this because I'm called to do it" or "I won't do it because I'm not called to do that job." Whereas before, I allowed myself to be worked to burnout. But I have more compassion for hurting people than I ever had and less of a judgmental attitude.

At this point you've had a lot of things resolved. Do you have any regrets?
If I had my "druthers," I never would have married my husband; I never would have left the church. If it had meant staying single, I would have stayed in it and stayed teaching because now I'm not teaching. I was one semester away from being vested for retirement, so I don't have my retirement, and I'm in my late fifties and looking back.

But actually, I think, in terms of the kind of work I can do for God now, I'm probably more valuable to Him in a lot of ways than I was before. So I figure He has some really exciting things for me to do. And I'm looking forward to the adventures.

Questions
1. What are some realistic ways we can teach young people to find a mate who is spiritually compatible?

2. Church members who fall into difficulties such as adultery or abuse cannot handle these problems alone. Who should a church member turn to as a first step to getting help? Does every member of your church know who to turn to?

3. Is it realistic to have a policy in the church whereby pastors and congregational leaders pursue all members who seem to be drifting from the church and stay in touch with them regularly for life?

4. Why do members in trouble sometimes go to other members, looking for the powerful, affirming love they could find in Jesus? Do we not teach that Jesus loves them much more than any members could?

5. Is it realistic to expect Seventh-day Adventists to model themselves on Jesus? Can we succeed if we don't?

Chapter 2

Bud

**early sixties, married, furniture-
building business owner**

**What was your first experience with the
Seventh-day Adventist Church?**

Mom and Dad were not real good Adventists when
I was little, but they were Adventists. They got better. I was born and raised in a small town in the sticks.
I had a really happy childhood there. A lot of hard
work because we were sharecroppers, but a happy
childhood. I had to be kept out of school sometimes to
get the crops in. I had a lot of chores.

When I was thirteen, Mom and Dad sold what few
possessions they had, and we moved to a city in the
Midwest. There were five of us kids, and I was next
to oldest. They wanted to be where they could give us
a Christian education because they knew they
couldn't afford to send us away.

I was baptized when I was twelve. After we moved, I
never did get along real well. My grades weren't good,
and I didn't get along with the teachers or the kids. I

worked hard, milked cows night and morning in eighth grade, plus going to school. But I just fell apart and grew away from the church. Never did settle in. When I was seventeen, I made the decision to leave home.

One of the worst decisions I ever made in my life was not to have anything to do with God. I just went out into the world and did my own thing.

I think I probably had a learning disorder of some kind. I don't feel I'm stupid, but my seventh- and eighth-grade teacher pegged me as retarded, and it took me years to get over that. I'm very successful in my business now, and I don't have a high education, but I'm not retarded.

Do you think when you got baptized you became a Christian?

I remember the event real well, and it was a good feeling, and I was sincere. But you know, I had a lot of growing to do yet, and really, there was no one to help with that part, I don't feel. That was the year the church school in my little home town closed down, and we went to public school—rode horseback about three miles.

Do you think that affected the way you went in future years?

I don't think so. I was happy there. I don't remember anything negative about it except it wasn't a Christian education. It was the first time evolution came up; I never really knew what it was until that point. That put a doubt in my mind that shouldn't have been there. No one explained it to me.

What did you think of God at that time?

You know, thinking back on it, I don't know. Must not have been a big impression. I'm not real sure.

No one told you much about Him?

Well, we went to church. I remember that real well, and I did believe in God. I remember thinking about heaven. Mom and Dad did read some stories to us and had worships. My baptism meant a lot to me.

How long were you away from the church?

I met my wife twenty-five years ago, and I came back into the church then. But I never did get serious. I'd try and then go out on the deep end again.

I became an alcoholic, and that controlled my life more than I realized. The devil had a hold of me. I'd come back to church, but it's a hard road getting back. Once you get out there in the world, there's a lot of fun out there, but it's only for a short time, and after a while you're sick and tired of being sick and you want to come back. But you're hooked.

I'd quit smoking for a while, and that was hard on me. And then I'd get smoking again and get to drinking again. It was just a constant battle.

So did you have much contact with the church all those years?

From when I was eighteen when I left home, from that point on, and I married my first wife, we didn't go to church. I was thirty-eight when I married my present wife. She is a good Christian gal.

On account of my drinking, me and my first wife split up, and she wouldn't take me back because it happened too many times. So I went into treatment and went to live with my sister and started a business. I was living in her basement. She's an Adventist, and I went to church with her, and that's how I met my wife that I have now.

I was rebaptized in the church then, but it didn't

last. Bless my wife, she's stuck with me, no matter the trouble I gave her over the years. I've been in alcohol treatment at least seven or eight times. I've lost count of them. Addictions were really hard on me. I was smoking, and I was just so addicted to it.

I colporteured. I came back into the church, and I was top salesman in a four-state area. I did that two different times, you know, trying to get back into the church. Then the alcohol would get a hold of me again, and I'd go off the deep end.

Did anyone from the church come and talk to you?

Oh yes. It seemed like when you went off the deep end, drinking again, they more or less left you alone; but I remember when I was in the church and they knew I'd had problems in the past, they'd say, "If you ever have any problems, just come to us. We're your friends."

But when the time comes when you're tempted, when you get that stinking thinking, you have to talk to another alcoholic who's been there. But you don't want to talk to anyone, and you won't. The thinking just gets worse until you do go back to drinking.

Did you go to Alcoholics Anonymous?

Yes I did. For three years. That's what sobered me up, and that's what's kept me sober. I'm in deep with the church now. I think AA did its thing for me, and they believe in God, but not the same way I think you should, so I feel I'm better off with the church.

How long have you been back as a full member of the church?

About seven years ago I was completely sober and was going to church. But I wasn't a member. I smoked, but I was sober. I didn't feel it was a priority to quit smoking then because of the alcohol problem. Then we moved again, and I did want to quit smoking and join the church. I just kept fighting it—I'd quit for a month or two and then start back in. I had a hard time with it.

Finally my attitude changed or something, because I made up my mind there wasn't going to be an option to smoke, no matter how bad I was tempted or how sick I felt. Once I got that in mind, when I was tempted, I could throw it out easier. I went to an Adventist stop-smoking program three times. And I finally got it with the Lord's help.

Do you think you had to come to the point where God was calling you, and it was the right time?

I used to hate guys who would tell how they just quit smoking. It was harder for me to quit smoking than to quit drinking. They'd say, "Ah, when I decided to quit, I just threw the pack up on the mantel and just forgot about it." It wasn't that easy; I couldn't do it. It's one of the hardest things I ever did.

What effect did all this have on your family?

I have two children from my first wife and two from my second. I have a son and daughter from my first wife. My daughter has never really had any experience or teachings of the church—maybe gone four or five times to church in her life. Not religious at all. She believes that being a good person is all you need to do.

My son from my first wife came to live with us when he was twelve. He's seen a lot of my bad times. But I wasn't the type of person that drank all the time, you know, only in spurts. I was always able to support my family. When the kids were little, my present wife didn't work and I supported them. We weren't rich, but they didn't do without anything. My oldest son was baptized when we had him in church school at thirteen. He went to self-supporting school for four years, and he liked it real well. It was his choice, instead of regular academy.

Right now we're concerned about him because he's quit going to church, and his wife, who went to the same self-supporting school, is a good Christian. He doesn't want to send the kids to church school. It's not important to him right now.

So we raised three boys, me and my present wife. We kept them in church school, even though I never got my life straight enough to be a church member. I guess my wife always had faith in me some way.

Both of my two younger sons went away to academy, and they didn't get along. They got kicked out of every academy they went to, and they were starting to mess with drugs at that point. Finally they just wanted to go to public school, and we didn't have much choice.

My youngest son was just baptized yesterday. I tell you, it's really an answer to prayer. Since he went on a mission trip with us, he quit smoking and drinking, and he hasn't missed a Sabbath at church since. He's not the same kid he was. It's hard to believe it. He gave a beautiful testimony yesterday, and it touched everybody's heart. There were a lot of tears.

My third son is not coming to church. When he was eighteen and he wanted to work for us, I told him, "Son, you can't work for us and do drugs, and you can't live at home and do drugs." He kept trying to tell me he wasn't. I said, "OK, son, let's go down and get a drug test, because I think you are. If we go and get a test and it proves me wrong, then I owe you a big apology." But, no, he wasn't going to get a test, and he moved out instead.

It wasn't two or three weeks and he was in trouble with the law. He ended up, at eighteen, getting a ten-year prison sentence, and for three-and-one-half years we stood behind him and visited him all the time. Tried to get his sentence shortened. We talked to the district attorney because he'd never been in trouble with the law before. He got out after three-and-one-half years.

He's going to college now, and he works for us now. He doesn't drink, and I think his heart has been softening up a little bit over time. He's a hard worker, getting almost straight As in college and working part time. Maybe he'll turn around. The Holy Spirit will have to do it.

Have you learned any principles from your experience?

I've got to live every day and ask the Holy Spirit to help me every day and surrender myself every day. If I don't, if I miss a day, I can feel myself sliding and starting to head toward the deep end again. It's a day-to-day thing. I learned from AA to live for today and not tomorrow. Your sobriety is today, and you have to live one minute at a time, one hour at a time. I've got my worship area at home, and I spend time in praying and studying a little bit just by myself. That's the only way to start my day. I surrender right there and ask the Holy Spirit to help get me through the day.

I have a business I started six years ago. I wasn't a church member then, but I made up my mind I wanted to pay tithe and be faithful about it, not fret over it, but do it with joy. And I did. The Lord has blessed me in my business. Of course, we've worked hard at it. We've been able to pay for my youngest son's drug treatments, which he couldn't have gotten otherwise. We were able to go be with him at family counseling. We could visit my third son in the penitentiary often and stay there and be a support for him. And we've been going on mission trips a lot.

What advice would you give to people outside the church?

I don't feel like I'm the type of person to be giving someone else advice [laughs]. I think they have to make decisions themselves. I'm telling you my experience and what I need. I'm staying sober one day at a time with God, with Jesus, and the Holy Spirit. That's the only way I can do it.

Questions

1. Can the Adventist church do more to help substance abusers before they get sober or conquer an addiction?

2. How should we react to a member who slides back into old habits?

3. How long should we pray for and care for a lapsed member who has backslidden over and over for many years?

4. What obligations do Adventist schools have to help at-risk students? Should such students always be removed to prevent corruption of the school? Can they be reclaimed?

5. Many children of Adventists get baptized between ten and thirteen. Does the Adventist Church minister effectively to new, young Christians? In what ways could we do a better job of building a firm spiritual foundation for them?

Chapter 3

Lee Ann

midtwenties, married, mother, homemaker

Tell me about yourself.

I grew up in a small town and still live there. I am married and have two children, a two-year-old boy and a two-month-old boy.

Were you raised as a Seventh-day Adventist?

Yes. When my grandmother became a Seventh-day Adventist, my mother became one, and I became one too. So I grew up in an Adventist home. My father wasn't an Adventist, so it was kind of half and half.

What about education?

I went to kindergarten and half of first grade in a public school. And the rest of the first grade up to fourth, I went to a Seventh-day Adventist school. And after that I went to public schools.

So you didn't go to academy or an Adventist college?

I had wanted to but didn't go to an Adventist academy.

You went to church regularly as a child and through your high school years?

Yes. We lived in my hometown until I was seven and then moved to a smaller town, and so I lived there until I got married and moved away.

Early on, was there something that tied you to the church?

No, not really. My mother made me go to church. As a child I enjoyed going to church because I had a lot of friends and I enjoyed the social aspect. They had sled-riding parties, and we were always doing things and going places. So I enjoyed that part of church activities, as most children do. But as I grew older and went to public school, I wanted to do things with my school friends on Sabbath. And since there weren't any Adventists my age, church was always a drag for me.

Would you say you had a real Christian experience as a young Adventist?

Oh yes. You know, the people make the church, and to me they were everything. You don't realize how much impact they have on those who come into the church. That same feeling is what I had when I was young and having fun—that people cared about me.

But in high school I was at a stage most teenagers go through. You just want to be on your own, rebellious, and you don't like anything your parents like. My mother would say, "Just wait till you have kids; they're going to be just like you."

Would you say that you were a truly converted Christian when you were baptized?

No. I wasn't. I got baptized because it was the right thing to do, what everybody expected of you. Even people who have been devout Christians—for instance, our Sabbath School teacher. To me she is just about as good a Christian as you can get. And she said that when she was young and got baptized it didn't mean the same to her as when she was older.

But I made the decision myself. I felt it was something I had to do.

Did you attend church regularly when you got into high school?

I still came to the church regularly. But since I was always involved in a lot of activities at school, I would tell Mom we had weekend trips, and since I was an officer in one of the organizations, I would say, "Mom, you know I want to go and you can't force me not to."

And she would just give up and say, "Go."

There was a couple of times when I missed church because of that. But other than that, I would go to church.

What led you away from the church?

When I turned eighteen I got married and thought I was enjoying life. I was going out and doing things I had never done before. I would go to Atlantic City. Of course, I was supposed to be twenty-one, but I somehow looked older than eighteen. I would gamble and do what I wanted, and people treated me like an adult. So I was doing worldly things that kept me away from going to church.

Your husband was not an Adventist?

No. I had come back to church for a little while when we were married, and I was back into reading the Bible. The Holy Spirit was always working on me. I don't know why, but He was. I tried bringing my husband to the church, but his mother kept saying, "Oh, you don't want to go there, come to my church." She had a great influence on him, and he listened to her.

He had been coming with me for a while. Eventually he stopped coming for weeks, and I gave up on him.

Your marriage broke apart then?

Yes. We were married for about a year and a half.

Then what did you do?

I got into all kind of problems.

How long were you out of the church?

After I left my husband, I was out for about three years.

While you were away from the church, did anybody call you?

Many church members tried getting hold of me. But I was really in a bad situation. I was living with someone who was not my husband. I had my own apartment. Everyone saw and knew what I was doing. Some of the church members were my friends. They were like close family to me. So I would call the Pathfinder leaders, and we'd get together. They had kids and would go on a bike ride along the river. And this was like on every other Sabbath.

But you weren't going to church?

I would see them on Saturday nights when we'd

all go out for pizza or some place like that, and we'd talk over dinner. We did this quite often. But it was never like a Sabbath social; it was just socializing. Other than that, I didn't have much contact with anyone when I was out of the church.

Did any of those people ever say, "Come on, Lee Ann, come back to church"?
They told me they missed me at church.

How about your parents?
My mom would ask me to come to church, but she never forced the issue. But she would comment on a lot of things I was doing. She would say, "You know that's not the right thing to do." And I knew I was wrong.

Did any of the pastors or the elders visit you?
Yes, they did. When I left my first husband, I was already dating Fred. The pastor came and talked with me. He told me they would have to take my name off the church books because of what I had done. And I just said, "Do what you've got to do."

That was the visit I got from a pastor. Other than that, no efforts were made by any other pastors or church elders.

Did they take your name off the church books?
No. He said something to my mother about it, I guess. And she had said to him, "Well, if you are going to take her name off, then maybe you ought to go through the names of all the members and look at all their sins and start taking some more names off the book." I guess that made him change his mind.

But I knew I was wrong, definitely wrong. And this

was kind of a blow to me. Nobody likes to be told they are wrong. Even when they are wrong. That's the way I felt.

What happened next?

Well, the three years when I lived with Fred, before I got married to him, were torture. I still loved my husband, but I was dating somebody else. And I was going through a lot of severe emotional problems. Fred kept saying that I was severely depressed, because I would go for two weeks feeling very depressed, and I wouldn't want to get out of bed or do anything. Other times I was really happy, and he just didn't understand me at all.

During those three years I started drinking—heavy drinking. I also started smoking. At that time Fred was drinking, so he didn't mind my drinking so much as the smoking. But I never did other drugs.

Meanwhile, my ex-husband was harassing me. He would drag me to court over and over and wouldn't leave me alone. He also tried to run me off the road. He followed me around. If I was at a restaurant, he'd see me and sit near the window and watch me. At that time I was on some kind of nerve medication, and I was really paranoid. Sometimes I took five or six pills at once.

Everywhere I went I would look behind me and would see him following me. He would light firecrackers outside the house and would do all kinds of stuff. Stuff you wouldn't even believe anybody would do. And the police weren't doing anything.

What turned that around?

Well, I got over my ex-husband. But I realized it was wrong for me to cheat on him by living with Fred.

It seemed that Fred was a God-send. He's been very supportive. He put up with everything that went on during those three years. All the fits that I threw and the times I stayed with my ex-husband—it's a miracle.

In spite of all these things, Fred stuck with me. He really truly loves me, and this is what keeps me going on a daily basis. And this is what helped my children and me to come out of all the miseries.

So how did you get back into an Adventist church?

Fred and I were married, and he knew I wanted children. I realized that children need some Christian background. I had a lot of good times when I was growing up in the church. Even before I got pregnant, I told Fred I didn't want the children to go to public school. I wanted them to go to private school. And Fred said that was fine.

Did he know what you were talking about?

Well, I think he did. I also told him, "I want the children to go to the Seventh-day Adventist Church, not to your church." He didn't mind, and he never ever questioned my beliefs.

Though I had not always lived an Adventist way of life, I knew that the Seventh-day Adventists were right. So I told Fred, "When we have kids, I want our children to be Seventh-day Adventists, and I want to raise them in the church and send them to church school." Fred was very cooperative when I said that to him. And so I kind of went back to the church mainly for my children, not for myself.

But when I started going back right after I got pregnant, everyone was so receptive, and I felt as if I was being welcomed like the prodigal son. I knew everybody still loved me and still cared for me. When I was pregnant, they even had a baby shower for me.

And while I was out of the church, a couple of new members had come in. I guess they must have joined right after I left the church. Even though they didn't know me, they still came for the baby shower. And when I went back to the church, they indicated they had missed me for years even though they didn't know me. And that was really what brought me back to the church. I was welcomed with open arms.

There were some who knew what had happened in my life and looked down on me, yet most of them were happy that I was back. So that's what brought me back to the church—the people.

How did it happen that your husband was baptized? Did you make that happen?

No, I didn't. It just happened. With my first husband, I always had to push him. The more I pushed, the more he went away. But when I asked Fred, "You want to come to church with me? I'd like you to come," a couple of times when he was off work, he came with me. And I said if he wanted to come again, that was fine. I never pushed him.

We talked about religion sometimes, and I said to him, "You know, it's going to confuse our children." Because when he was off on Sundays, he would go to church with his dad. So I said, "The children will not understand why Daddy goes to church on Sundays and Mommy goes to church on Saturdays." Then I said, "We need to have one religion, and I am not changing."

So he started coming to church with me. He took Bible studies, and he started realizing, "Wow, I didn't know all these things—like there are pagan churches and the things that happened in the Dark Ages." Like what we read in *The Great Controversy*. He had no clue that things like that ever happened. The more he learned, the more I saw a change in him. I also prayed for him, but I never pushed.

What did you learn during your three years away from the church? And what is it like now?

Well, since I am back into the church, I have been much happier than I was in my entire life. I know I did a lot of things I shouldn't have. But I am truly happy to be back.

What are your goals now that you are back in the church?

My kids are so young, and they take up so much of my time right now. There are so many things I would like to do. I am trying to get involved in the church a little and do something for the church because there is nothing in the church for the kids. That's how it was when I was growing up, and that's why I hated Sabbath.

I try to do something for the little kids, like a video about nature and things like that for Sabbath afternoon or evening. And if it is not too cold, then we go out for a walk. I want my kids to grow up and enjoy the Sabbath and not be bored.

Usually by the end of the week I am exhausted, and sometimes I do take a nap on Sabbath. Right now my children are small, and I haven't done much for them. But as they grow up, I want them to have something. So in order to do that, I need to make plans for their Sabbath activities.

I want my kids to live an active life. I want them to enjoy camping, biking, hiking, or anything they want to try. I want to let them live a meaningful life. I may be broke financially, but I want my kids to have some pleasant activities on Sabbath afternoon.

What would you say to people who left the church but may have no intention of returning?

Well, if they were in the same situation that I was in, I would say to them, "Look at what you are doing. Does it bring happiness?" I was getting deeper in a hole, and I was not able to get out of it. I had good times. I am not saying I was miserable the whole time. But most of the time I was depressed, I was angry at everybody, and I lied to everybody. And because of it I had to go through a lot of torture. If I had been on the right track to begin with, I would not have had to go through all this.

What about the people who are in the church, the ones you grew up with and who are still there, especially the older members? What would you say to them when they see a young person drifting away?

Just love them. I am not criticizing. Maybe I am. Being back in the church, I have seen members who push people out because they've got new members. They don't care for those coming back to the church because of what they were doing before.

People in the church need to watch their actions and words. That is very important. Because when I first went back there for a Revelation seminar, some people in the church made me feel that I should not be there. I felt very uncomfortable.

There was this one lady in particular. We had new member classes, and on this lady's class door was written, "If you come late, don't bother coming in." So if you are coming off the street or even a former member coming back and you saw that sign, instead of going in you'd walk out. The first impact is so great that the person would have a hard time coming back.

Another time the church had to vote something a new pastor wanted to change when he first came. Some didn't mind this change. But the older members didn't like it. So they went up to the pulpit and spoke up. And here I am, coming back into the church and bringing my husband, too, at that time. I said to myself, "Man, who is running the church?" Sometimes certain members in the church don't realize what impact they have on people who come there. They have to be careful with their words and actions.

Would you say that you and Fred have been welcomed into the church family?
Yes.

What advice do you have for new members?
Sometimes you get spiritually weak even though you are rebaptized, and I am at that point now because I am so tied up with my children from morning till night. I get so involved with my children that I don't take enough time for God.

I would say to the new members, "If you become weak, don't give up. Just get up and keep going." They say you need to bring people closer to Christ and give Bible studies and right now, I wonder what God thinks when He looks at me because I don't make time for Him as I should.

You have two little Bible studies right here at home, and sometimes that is the most effective thing a young mother can do—to teach her children to love Jesus.

I am trying. Though at times I just don't feel like it. I feel tired all the time, and if I have five minutes to read the Bible or anything, I cannot absorb what I read. Sometimes I feel like I am so far away from God. I know He is with me always. He has been there with me from the time I was born until this day. He has never left me, and that is the reason I have come back to the church.

Thinking back over my past and the things I did, like drinking and smoking, the gambling and cheating on my first husband—God never left me. He was always there for me. He has done things for me no human being has ever done. I know He loves me.

Chapter 4

Jeff

**late twenties, married, factory
worker**

Have you always been an Adventist?

Ever since I can remember. I was in the church as a
kid. My parents were Christians, and my father was a
Seventh-day Adventist. I grew up in the church and went
to Adventist schools for elementary and high school.

**Do you think you were truly converted when
you first joined the church?**

At that time, it was probably something that I took
for granted. I was a Christian and, yes, I believed in
God and prayed every night. I thought I had a good
relationship with the Lord, but I never took it seriously as I should have. It was something I grew up
with, and yet I just never knew how much it was supposed to mean to me. I should have been more serious about that. What I was taught was always inside, but I kept pushing it aside.

Did you have a good academy experience?

I would say that I had a fair academy experience, especially since I had a lot of friends. Actually, they are all gone now, except for one. I keep in contact with him. I just went to my first alumni meeting— my tenth-year alumni meeting, the first one I ever attended. I got to see a lot of old friends, and it was really nice. Some of them were still in the church.

But it was in academy that I started to go downhill. I just couldn't put up with all the rules. I got kicked out three times. I'm not proud of that. I wasn't allowed to march with my graduating class. That left a kind of sour taste with me.

Once I moved back home from academy, I left all my Christian friends there. A lot of them were going off to college and I wasn't, so I just lost contact with everyone. Even my friends at my home church were away at school, and since I was older than most of them, they were still away at school for the next two or three years. So really, there was no one for me, no friends in church. No girlfriends either [laughs].

What led you away from the church?

Number one, I was probably looking for a girlfriend [laughs]. There were no Christian girls that I was really interested in—none in my church. I was about the only young person there most of the time. Well, this led me to look at non-Christian girls for dating. But that was a hundred percent different. I mean just the things you are interested in. I really didn't fit in with that crowd.

Without much of a choice for friends, I had to adapt and make myself fit in with people outside the church. They definitely didn't become like me; I did the changing. They already had their friends. And if I dated someone, I would have to go with their group.

What sort of life did you have away from the church?

The first thing I started doing was to listen to rock 'n' roll music. I didn't think it was wrong to listen to that. To me, just listening to the music wasn't bad, but it eventually led me from one thing to another and later introduced me to a completely different lifestyle. You know, drinking, partying, and things like that.

I had a girlfriend but not a steady one. It was more like just dating a bunch of different girls and stuff like that. I started slowly with drinking, you know, social drinking. I really never liked it and hated to do it. But if I was going to have friends, I had to be one of the crowd. It was like, the more you do it, the more you don't think about it. As far as drugs are concerned, I never got into that.

I wouldn't consider myself a kid, because I was twenty years old. I guess I am the only one to be blamed though. I did feel some pressure from some of the girls I dated and some of their friends, but it was my own choice.

So that's how I gradually drifted and started living a worldly life. I stopped going to church. And it doesn't take a long time for the devil to get a hold on you and change your life if you don't have a relationship with God. I realized where I was headed. I knew whose side I was on and never liked being on the side that wasn't happy. I knew I was going to hell, and that made me miserable. I hated the way I was living my life, but I didn't realize I needed Jesus for true happiness.

How long were you out of the church?

I lived at home with my parents for about three years after I was back from academy. I went to church

off and on when they made me. I was out of the church
for about eight years.

Church wasn't "cool." Church was boring, not fun,
and full of old people. I quit going, and the devil had
his chance with me, because I didn't have Jesus in
my life.

**Did you have any contact with the church
while you were away?**

No. I really never had much contact with any
Adventists. My parents and our next-door neighbors—
they, too, are Adventists—whom I rarely saw then were
always around, but I kind of separated myself from them
and from the church. During weekends I was doing a
lot of running around. I wasn't uncomfortable around
Adventists. My parents stayed as close as I would let
them. A couple of different pastors came to the house to
visit me, but nothing ever went well.

During most of the time I was away, my parents
and I never really got along. I was an angry person,
so I really didn't have a good relationship with them.
They are my parents, and I love them, but we didn't
see things the same way. I finally moved out of my
parents' house and got my own place.

**Did you think about the church or church
members while you were away?**

Sometimes. I knew they were right, and I also knew
I would eventually come back. But I was a little con-
fused for a while. For at least four or five years I didn't
think about the church so much. But during the last
four years, mainly the last three years, I've really been
convicted about my life. I believe that the Holy
Spirit—and my parents, who were pretty understanding—led me back to church.

Did any other people try to influence you to change your life?

Yes. I met this guy at work. His name is Danny. At the beginning we didn't get along much when I started working there. But we eventually became friends, and he helped me as far as getting a better job there. I guess he saw some qualities in me he figured would be useful in the company. If it weren't for him, I wouldn't be a spray painter, which is a good paying job. In fact, it's the best paying job where I work. I was really happy to get that job.

Danny and I became friends, and we did a lot of fishing together. He is a very good Christian and goes to the Assembly of God church. He would share with me what he knew, even though I didn't want to talk about it. He never talked about church doctrines, but he wanted me to get back to church. He would say things like "What do you think? Where you gonna' end up? Heaven or hell?"

And I would say, "I don't know where I'm going. But I know I have lived a wrong life."

Then he would say, "Then why don't you change?"

While we were fishing he would talk about God's love for man. But it would only be real brief, because he knew I wouldn't want to listen to him if he was preaching. But he was my friend.

When did you first think of going back to church?

During the last three years away from the church, there was a feeling inside me, and I knew that eventually I wanted to come back. I knew it was right, and I knew that God wanted me back. It seemed as though I was being convicted by the Holy Spirit to "Straighten yourself out." Sometimes in my bed at night I would just lie there and think.

Finally I couldn't put it off any longer. My conviction got stronger each day. I knew I was on a dead-end road. It seemed as if God had to let me see enough so I would come back to Him.

I had been struggling—trying to quit drinking and get away from tobacco. One Friday night I started praying. I had prayed every day—even while I was doing things I knew I shouldn't. But this time it was different. I pleaded for help. I didn't sleep all night. It was kinda' like wrestling with God. I wanted Him to win. And He did.

I got up early Saturday morning and got dressed. I got in my car and started driving around. At eleven o'clock I was in front of the Adventist Church, and I knew my parents were inside. And I decided I was going back to church after being away for eight years. I parked my car and went in.

What kind of a response did you get?
My parents always sit almost at the front on the left side of the church. I walked up to the end of the pew where they were sitting and sat down with them. When they saw me, both of them were shocked, and tears came to their eyes.

That Sabbath, a great peace came over me. And I went home from church that day determined that I wouldn't drink or chew tobacco ever again. And I haven't. God has taken all that away.

I knew that was where I belonged, so I went to church that Sabbath. The next Sabbath Mona went with me, and we've been going to church ever since.

Tell me about Mona.
I met Mona about three years ago. She's a great

person! Right away, I felt comfortable with her. She never had any bad habits like drinking, and she was not trying to cool me down like everyone else was. She didn't argue with me. She gave me space, and I had a chance to calm down. I had a chance to evaluate myself.

Even though Mona didn't have a Christian background, she knew right from wrong. She never liked me drinking or using tobacco or cussing and things like that. So I told her I would try to quit.

From the beginning she helped me. And once I calmed down I think it was easier for me to take inventory of my life. So Mona has been a great influence in my life. I wanted to spend my life with her from the time I first saw her.

I realized I wasn't doing right, and I knew I had to have my life straightened out. We were living together when I started to become a Christian again, and I knew that I didn't deserve to have my name on the church books. I wanted the minister to marry us, but he couldn't marry an Adventist to non-Adventist. All those years I guess I was still a member even though I never had anything to do with the church. When the minister said he couldn't marry an Adventist to a non-Adventist, I took my name off the books so he could marry us. So we got married.

I was kind of nervous coming back to church, but as soon as I walked in the front door I knew I was welcome. As soon as I walked into the church I considered myself a member again. And people were nice and friendly. And when Mona saw that I was welcomed with open arms, that's one thing that really helped her.

Now we both are taking Bible studies and very shortly she intends to be baptized, in fact within a month or so, I will be rebaptized, and she will be baptized. We'll do it together.*

Another thing that helped was the way people treated Mona. The church people were very friendly to her. A lot of them knew we were living together. When the church people found out that we were really going to get married, some of them got together and had a shower for Mona. She was really happy that they cared enough to do that. And I was happy too.

What if Mona hadn't come to church with you? What if she hadn't become a Christian?

I would have come back to the church anyway, because I knew that's where I belonged. Since I've been back, I've had peace in my life, and I've been happy for the first time in a long time.

How has your life changed since you came back to church?

Now I have a new relationship with God. I know it will grow after a while if I stay in constant contact with the Lord. It's something you have to nurture, I found out. Just like a marriage.

I just came back to the church about six months ago and started reading the Bible from Genesis on, and now I've read the whole Bible from beginning to end. I am reading the Bible every night and also reading other Christian books. I am reading a lot every day and trying to keep a good relationship with the Lord. I have also started going to church every Saturday. If it's possible, I would like to go to church on Wednesday nights, too, since it is halfway through the week. I feel like having an extra feast for my hungry soul.

My parents are so happy because I came back to

the church. It has had a great impact on them because it definitely made their faith grow in the Lord. It gave them an extra boost and has revived the fire within them.

What have you learned about yourself through all this? Do you have any regrets?

I never took Christianity very seriously. I just went to academy. I really never wanted to go away from my parents. But I did. And I met a lot of Christian friends there. But once I left academy, for eight years I was miserable, and I never knew why.

I am ashamed of my previous life. I put myself through a hard time. I was just living a worldly life when what I needed was Christ in my life. It seems now that I have Him back in my life, I am perfectly content. I really never knew back then that I wasn't on God's side. I was blind to that until my prayer was answered.

I learned that Christians don't get breaks from Satan. Without God, Satan will win every time. Since I was not strong in God, Satan had me dancing over the flames I couldn't see. But God had better plans for my life. I didn't intentionally choose Satan's side. It just happened.

It's hard to believe that God will take me back as a sinner and forgive me and grant me the gift of eternal life with Him. He has given me back my life. The greatest gift I've got right now is that my wife is becoming a Seventh-day Adventist too.

What are your goals now that you are back in the church?

I definitely want to remain an Adventist. I know I want to walk closer with the Lord. I want to live for Him. And I want to help out in any way I can. Like anything in the church I can do—maybe be a deacon in the church.

I have a lot of catching up to do. I'm rusty. I was out eight years, but now I'm learning. Mona helped out in the Vacation Bible School last summer, and I helped her a couple of nights.

What would you say to people who have left the church and seem to have no intention to return?

I wish they would understand there is nothing out there. It's just a bad deal out there in the world. You are not going to get any satisfaction from the world. The only satisfaction you are going to get is to get back to the church and be in communion with the Lord. I tried it out there, but there was no true happiness in it for me. And there is no way they can possibly be happy, even though they think they are.

I never wanted to be miserable, and I never realized what I was missing. I never realized that the Lord will give me happiness. It sounds strange but, you know, I was in it for happiness out there and just couldn't find it. It seems all of sudden I woke up, and I just realized at the snap of my fingers that I wanted to come back to the church. I really enjoy talking to Christians now, and I love to go to Sabbath School classes and learn. It's nice to be around other Christians.

So I would say, "Open your eyes. Evaluate your life and ask yourself, 'Am I really happy?' Open your eyes and accept the free gift of eternal life that Jesus Christ gives."

What would you say to those who have just become Christians?

I think they should be happy they got themselves

out of the world and got themselves into good churches where people are straightforward and honest, where there is good teaching, and where people really love the Lord. They are lucky to have found a church like that. I would tell them, "Let the Holy Spirit lead you. And when things get rough—and they will—get down on your knees and pray." That's what I have to do.

Questions

1. Does the Adventist Church need a safety net of intentional ministry to young members in churches with a small number of young adults?

2. What should we do about the prevalence of young adults in churches with few Adventist peers from which to choose a mate?

3. Could we shorten the time that some ex-members are gone by advising them or intervening in some way? What might be the down side of "helping"?

4. How can we better communicate the fact that the gospel is good news?

5. In what ways could we direct the effective testimony of reborn Adventists toward helping former or fringe members with their spiritual lives?

* Jeff and Mona were baptized in November 1996.

Chapter 5

Cherie

**fifties, married, mother,
grandmother, nurse**

Did you grow up an Adventist?
Yes and no. My mother was an Adventist, and my
father was a Roman Catholic, so I grew up in half an
Adventist home. I grew up knowing Adventist principles, and I thank God for my mother's perseverance
for sticking with her convictions. It wasn't that easy
for her.

At what point did you become an Adventist?
I would say it was when I was originally baptized. I guess when I was about eleven or twelve
years old.

**Did you understand what you were doing
when you were baptized?**
Yes. I really felt that I did. I think I loved the Lord
then. I may have not understood everything, but I loved
the Lord the way an eleven- or twelve-year-old would.

Did you leave the church as a young person?

Yes, I did. I grew up in a very poor home, and since my father was a Catholic, he didn't see any need for a Christian education. So I went to public school for many years, and I sort of just blended in with the kids who were poor. It wasn't a big deal. But I had the opportunity to go to church school for the seventh and eighth grades. It certainly was a unique experience.

Most of the kids at this school were kind of rich, but not by today's standards. To me they seemed rich. In those days, they were definitely the elite of the crop. I tried to fit in with them, but it just didn't work. It was kind of a unique situation.

You felt like other people had more than you did?

I never felt I was good enough. No matter what I did. I remember one time when a doctor's wife wanted me to fit in. She was a lovely lady. There were several doctors who had kids in that school. She or her daughter invited me—I don't remember exactly who—to her home, and I was very excited. It was just the highlight of my life to get to go to their home. They had horses! And they had other things I could only dream of.

When I went to their house, everyone was very nice to me. But then one of the kids came and told me that their mother had made them invite me and that they really didn't want me to come. When I heard that, it really broke my heart. I really was hurt because I found out that those kids really didn't want me to be there. I felt I just wasn't part of that group, even though I went to school with them.

What happened that took you away from the church?

Things just went from good to bad. Probably a lot of it was my own insecurity. My growing up in insecurity and the treatment I got from some of the kids at school made me more insecure. Some of them tried to be good friends, but I wanted to blend in with that top group, and I just didn't make it. I got to the point where I was so hurt that I went out of the church because of it.

As a teenager, I started dating outside the church, and it caused a lot of grief at home. I was only seventeen when I got married, but when you are seventeen, you think you have lived a long time. You just think that nothing is ever going to change and that this is just the way life is.

And I came to a point in my life when I felt I didn't fit in anywhere, and I didn't want to have any part of the church. I felt hurt; I felt rejected. I felt unwanted, and I felt that these people didn't like me. That was the way I perceived it—and maybe I was wrong; maybe it was just my own insecurity. I can see that now, but as a child I couldn't. Even as a teenager, I couldn't figure all that out.

So I became engaged and was planning to get married. I remember riding over to one of the Adventist churches in the area and talking to the pastor. And the pastor said, "Cherie, we haven't seen you in church lately."

I said, "No, you will never see me in the church again."

And he said, "Well, we want you back."

Then I said, "Yeah, sure." I remember saying, "It will be a cold day in you know where before I will come back to church."

Then he said, "I know someday you will be back."

I laughed.

Well, I got married, and we moved to another state. We lived there for some time.

Did you have any contact with Adventists?

No. I didn't want any contact. I wanted to do all the wild and frivolous things everybody else did, including drinking and all that kind of stuff. I clearly remember a few incidents that indicated that I should be mending my ways.

For example, every time I drank, I became deathly ill. And another time when I was pregnant with my first child, someone mixed clam chowder and beer together and gave it to me to drink. As a result, I suffered for days. I did stuff I thought was wonderful and fun, but actually, it wasn't. I look back now and realize how empty my life was.

So you didn't marry an Adventist?

No, I didn't. I put my marriage and everything about it above God. But I really, truly feel that the Lord sent Frank to me. He is such a good person. God knew what He was doing. Yet I felt I was still missing something.

How did you get back to the church?

Well, there was something down deep inside me that brought me back to the church. First of all, I had a baby, and when it came time to christen this baby, I knew I couldn't do it. I couldn't bring myself to take that baby to the Methodist church to have him christened. I knew better. I knew that it wasn't a baptism. Everyone kept saying, "But it's just water, it won't hurt." And I kept saying, "No, no, I can't do that."

Then I went to a Baptist church. One Sunday out of the clear blue I dedicated my son to the Lord in the

Baptist church. After the service, the pastor asked me if I was joining the church. And I said, "No, I dedicated my child to the Lord, not to this church." But this meant a lot to me, to dedicate him to the Lord. That's the way I wanted it done. There was no Adventist church nearby, and I had no other way of dedicating my son—I didn't drive much and had no way of getting to any church at that time.

Did you want to go to an Adventist church?

I had thought about it several times. I remember thinking sometimes that I would like to go to church for at least one Sabbath. But I quickly put this thought away and didn't go. I didn't go back to an Adventist church till we moved back to my home state.

I know the Lord had His hands on us, moving us home. But He also had His hands on our getting back to church.

One day several months after we had moved back, I was in the grocery store and I heard my name yelled across the store. And I thought, *Who could that be?* And I saw this young man running across the store toward me. He came right up to me, threw his arms around me, and kissed me on the cheek. I looked up, wondering who this young man was, but I couldn't remember him.

Then he said, "You don't remember me, do you?"

And I said, "No, I don't." I was so shocked that I couldn't think straight. It turned out that he was one of those kids who had shunned me at the church school.

He asked me, "Where have you been? We've been wondering what happened to you."

He asked me if I was going to church. I said, "Well, I've been around. I'm married and have a couple of kids."

And he said, "We want you to come back to church."

I responded very bluntly, "There is no way I am coming back to the church. There is just no way I am coming back."

I didn't want to run into him again, so I changed my grocery shopping night. But the next time I was at the grocery store, the same thing happened. The same young man came running to me, threw his arms around me and said, "Oh, it's good to see you again. I was wondering if I was going to bump into you again."

That night I met his wife, who was there with him, and it was a pleasant occasion. She seemed very nice.

But I kept thinking, *He didn't even like me at school. Why is he so happy to see me now?* That happened about five times in a row. I kept changing my shopping day and even the time of day I went to the store, but every time for about five weeks, he was there. I kept thinking, *There's got to be a way of getting rid of him.* But there wasn't. I began to wonder if maybe Someone up there was making this happen.

About the fifth meeting he said, "Look, we meet in the school auditorium regularly; why don't you come over for just one Sabbath and make me happy."

I finally said, "OK. I'll just go for one week if you will stop meeting me at the grocery store."

This was the way I thought I could get rid of him. Well, that was it. I went that first Sabbath, and I started going to church from then on.

When you went to church, what kind of a reception did you get?

Actually, I think I grew up a lot during the time I was away. I got a very good reception. I felt at home. It was as if there was some kind of an inner peace there that I had not known for a long time. Ever since

I had been out of the church, there was something in
life I was missing, but I couldn't figure out what it
was. When I came back into the church, I made up
my mind that no matter what happened or who did
what, I would never, ever go out of the church again—
and the Lord had to be first in my life.

How did you get back into the congregation?
Well, to tell you the truth, it was a little while before I was rebaptized. I had told my husband about
running into this man who kept meeting me at the
store, and he finally met him. One day Greg asked us
if we both would like to take Bible studies. And my
husband reluctantly agreed.

One of the church elders and his wife came to our
house and gave us the Bible studies at that time. He
wasn't a regular pastor. He was a lay pastor. He and his
wife came and gave us Bible studies for quite a while,
and as a result, my husband and I were both baptized.

**Did you see any more of those old friends,
people you had gone to school with?**
Not really. But we became close friends with Greg
and his wife, and I really felt like I was at home when
I first went back.

What made you feel that way?
I really don't know. It was nothing you could put
your finger on. My life just felt more complete. I think
it was a little bit of everything.

I really have felt more at home where we go to church
now, to tell you the truth. Because it is a smaller church.
The church I grew up in was very large. There were
very nice people there, but you never felt like close family the way you do in our present church. I really feel at

home where we are now.

Over the years since coming back to the church, I've had a close relationship with God. And I've also learned a lot. I've grown up enough to know that no matter which church you go to, if you look at people, you are going to fail every single time. Because you can't look at anybody else and see God. Satan will use other people and use me to misrepresent God and His church.

So it wasn't people who brought you back, it was the Holy Spirit?

Definitely. It was the Holy Spirit working in my life. He used the same people who took me out of the church to bring me back. I think of all the people I could have run into at the grocery store who could have said, "Come over, we would like you to come to our church." But God used the same people who had turned me away from the church to bring me back.

Did you run into any problems with any of these people you had known when you went to school together? How did they respond to you as an adult?

Well, Greg was the only one I actually saw. I did go to the doctor's son's house once to pick up some things I had bought. That was soon after we had moved back home, before I saw Greg. The doctor's son asked, "Where did you go?" And we talked for a bit.

Mostly, I kept remembering how I felt when we went to school together—that nothing is ever going to change and that this is just the way life is. But when you get older, you find out that it's just a beginning. I just wish people could have been more compassionate toward me as I was growing up.

How long has it been since you came back into the church?

I came back about 1969, so it's been about twenty-eight years.

Do you have any goals for yourself and your family as far as church is concerned?

Before I tell you my goals, I want to talk about my regrets. My regrets are that when my son was little, I wasn't in the church; I think things would have been different for him. I didn't come back into the church until he was six or seven years old. And I think he got his values all mixed up at that time.

My main goal is to claim the promises of God and to see my children, grandchildren, and great-grandchildren in heaven. And I want to be more compassionate to people around me, to reach out to those who might be outside the fence now. I just want to let the Lord use me as He sees fit, wherever that is, whatever He wants me to do.

How do you respond to the newcomers in the church, who may feel they are outside the circle, so to speak?

I sometimes think we are too self-centered and not responsive to newcomers. And I think this is one of Satan's tools to distract us. We should be like God—accept the people just the way they are.

What would you like to say to people you know who've been in the church, have left, and have no plans to return?

Whatever I might say won't make much difference. It's a mean world out there. But I am happy for myself now. It's not that I have anything special, but because God is on my side. I know I am going to be OK. It doesn't mean I am perfect; it means I will try to do the right thing—but He is in charge.

And when you get out there and He is not there and you are not allowing Him to be there for you, you better watch out because there is a lot of hurt out there. During the time I was out in the world, I was hurt devastatingly, especially as a teenager. You are playing with dynamite.

What would you say to people who've been in the church all their lives?

I think in a way they are in a kind of dangerous situation. Sometimes you become placid, or you sort of just drift along, and you are satisfied and maybe take things for granted. I feel that way sometimes, and I can't accomplish much.

Sometimes I envy those who have never gone out of the church. At the same time, I would say, Don't be satisfied with what you have. Search for the true meaning of life and develop your personal relationship with God. God is in charge. He is right there, waiting. And He is willing to do anything for you. Just don't become too complacent.

What about new Adventists? What would you like to say to encourage them?

Hold on to that first love. And reach out, loving the Lord. Studying His word is really important to have a true relationship with Christ.

You left the church when you were a teenager. Would you say that you came back to the church because of your children?

I think the children were the tool. Knowing that I

wanted my children to grow up to be good people was the tool God used. But I think the foundation my mother laid and my father, too, in a sense, made me realize and think. My father never interfered with my mother when it came to my religious upbringing. It was just the love of God that made this possible. And I owe a lot to my aunt, who brought my mother into the church.

I have so much to be thankful for. I can't dwell on the negative. I have so much in the world that I can't even thank God enough.

What about your children? Are they in the church?

Well, both of our daughters have been divorced but have remarried and are in the church. It's unfortunate it happened that way, but I'm grateful they are in the church at this time.

My son is not. He is getting married soon, and his wife-to-be is an agnostic. I'm not happy about that, but she is a fine person who just hasn't had a chance to know the Lord yet. Maybe if we just love her, she will come to know the love of God. Just as He gave me my husband. She is really on the same level as I was at that time. But the Lord brought us both to Him, and that's what I am hoping and praying for my son and his bride.

You know, the Bible says, "Train up a child in the way he should go, and when he is old he will not depart from it." I reminded my son of that the other day and told him, "I am claiming that promise." And he just grinned.

Questions

1. How can church members become more aware of the effects of subtle discrimination? Should pas-

tors talk about it from the pulpit?

2. Cherie refers to the damage the world does to teenagers. Should we continue to pointedly warn teenagers, even if they don't seem to listen? Have we gradually stopped preaching to young people because they object? Because they annoy us?

3. In what ways might Cherie's church reach out to her son and his bride-to-be? How might the church support Cherie in her desire to see them baptized?

4. Greg persisted in his contact with Cherie to the point that she was willing to attend church just to get rid of him. Is this an appropriate approach to those who have left the church? Explain your answer.

Chapter 6

Tim

---

early thirties, married, magazine editor

What was your earliest experience of the SDA church?

I've often thought that Paul's description of himself as a Hebrew of the Hebrews applied to me in the Adventist sense. My mother was a second generation Adventist in England, so she grew up around Adventism all her life, and then, of course, I did too. My dad became a Christian in his midtwenties, and he became an Adventist before he met my mom, and before I came along obviously.

So in the first seventeen years of my life, I went to church, or was taken to church, *every* Sabbath year after year after year. My earliest memories are of going to church on Saturdays.

I was born in Watford, England, where to this day, several Adventist administrative offices and institutions are based. If there's an Adventist ghetto in England, it would be Watford.

We moved from Watford when I was two, but I had close ties to the town because my grandparents lived at Stanborough Park in Watford, where all those offices are, for many years afterward. We moved from Watford to Grantham because my dad was working for the Stanborough Press, the church's publishing house, at the time it moved up there. So even that early in my life my dad was a denominational employee.

Later my dad went back to college, became a teacher, and taught in public schools for a few years. When I was eleven, he and my mom, who had also trained to be a teacher, accepted jobs in Africa and became denominational employees again.

So you could say first of all that I was brought up in the routine of Adventism from birth. My mom had read a lot of Ellen White, especially just before I was born, so she based quite a bit of her life on what she read there. I would say she took advice from Ellen White that seemed to fit our circumstances and made sense in this day and age. I think she had good enough judgment to know what in Ellen White's advice to parents was more suitable to the nineteenth century and what was suitable to the 1960s.

So we had a fairly strict home that followed Adventist culture quite carefully. Strangely, my parents were not strict vegetarians. They both grew up eating meat, so we occasionally had it, mostly at restaurants. It was one thing that wasn't a conflict to them. I'm not sure why. They would never, ever have drunk alcohol or gone to a store on Sabbath or gone to a movie theater.

Grantham, the English town where I grew up, became something of an Adventist ghetto after the press moved there. It had one of the larger Adventist churches in England, with a school built on the side of it. I went to that school from day one of my schooling until I was ready for high school. I was surrounded by Adventist culture for five days of school and immersed in it on Sabbath. That pretty much describes every week of my life until I was about 20.

If anyone ever had a problem separating their identity as an individual person from their identity as a member of a subculture, it was me. I'm the poster boy for the Adventist child's identity crisis.

Do you consider that you became a converted Christian when you first joined the church?

When I was baptized into the church, I had decided it was the right time to do it. I realize now that I didn't understand what it means to be a Christian. I understood what it meant to join the church, and at the time I was baptized, I was quite willing and happy to not just conform but to conduct my life in a way that was in agreement with church doctrine and practice.

I did study the Bible and knew quite a lot about it. But for all the explanation and instruction I got, and I did get some good insight from teachers about what it really means to be a Christian, for some reason it didn't click in my mind, and I didn't actually begin experiencing being a Christian.

I think there are several reasons for this. One of them is that my parents didn't talk about it. This is a very odd thing to me, but my parents were quite willing to get into a screaming argument about the kind of music I was listening to (which caused them great agony), but I don't remember ever having a conversation where we defined what it means to be a Christian and the reasons for it. I don't know if it's because they didn't have reasons or simply that they never thought to express them. I suspect the latter, but I'll never know, since they're not around anymore.

So I'd have to say that I was not truly converted when I was baptized. It happened when I had just turned sixteen and I had come through many years of feeling that I was not drawn to religious things. Probably ever since I had gone to school at six years of age and become aware of Bible stories outside my home environment, I had been aware that I knew about these things and was not drawn to them and didn't particularly want to follow them.

When I was fifteen I began to think about joining the church. I suspect that it had something to do with the girl I was dating at the time because we had a serious relationship. By steps we worked toward doing the right thing in various areas of our lives, which was good. But it led me to study and accept things as truth without that key element—the fundamental ingredient of a Christ-centered life—knowing and experiencing God Himself.

What initially led you away from the church?

Shortly after I was baptized, the mother of the girl I was dating contracted leukemia and succumbed to it very quickly. That was a great challenge to both of us. I guess I was able to be a little bit of support to her at the time, but I didn't feel adequate to the task.

I had seen a fellow academy student (I went to Adventist academy all the way through high school years too) taken by leukemia just the year before, and all of us who had seen the first situation felt that this was another visitation of something horribly familiar.

This was very disturbing to me, but I think at the time this girl and I felt our faith was just what we needed and that we'd been led to the point of having faith so we could deal with whatever we had to. And this was the first big test.

A couple of months after that, this girl's father moved back to his home country from Africa, and the girl went with him, obviously. So we tried to have a bit of a long-distance relationship, which was very difficult because she was basically on the other side of the world from me.

A month after she left, I went back to England to attend the Adventist boarding school in Watford (of course). I had been back about two months when the principal of the school came to my room one evening. I had been out somewhere and came back; I couldn't find anyone. I wondered why no one was around. So I went to my room, and then the principal came and told me that my parents had been killed. Some terrorists had basically beaten them to death. It was extremely violent, and for my dad in particular, a horrifically slow death.

The principal brought the local Adventist doctor with him. They talked to me for a while, and the doctor gave me something to help me sleep.

So of course I had to deal with the whole situation of going back to Africa for the funeral of my parents and linking up with my brother, who's two years younger than me and was going to Adventist academy in Africa at the time.

I can't begin to describe the emotions that weigh on you in that kind of situation. But the thing about emotions is that after a long enough time, they wear off. So I would say it was not an emotional burden that affected my faith afterwards.

How far away did you go and for how long?
Before my parents were murdered, I had been read-

ing my Bible every day and had actually read quite far through it. I had started at the beginning before I left Africa and continued to read it every day at school in England. I continued to do this after I got back from my parents' funeral. I was liking what I was reading, but I wasn't aware that I didn't know how to make it work for me the way it's supposed to, the way God promises it will. I don't really understand why.

About two months after the funeral, I began skipping reading the Bible sometimes, and my attitude began to change. I didn't really notice it at first. My roommate at the Adventist boarding school thought of himself pretty much as an atheist, or at least an existentialist, reading Albert Camus novels and that kind of thing. So I began to pick up on some of this, not because this person was trying to lead me astray (far from it) but because I began to be sympathetic to that sort of thinking.

Someone I know who's older than me, whom I have great respect for, was quite angry about what had happened to my parents. And he said to me, "Where was God in this situation? Was He just playing Tiddley-Winks or something? He just wasn't there." I think it confirmed in his mind a lot of skepticism about God and God's role. That thought stayed with me, as a question, as to what on earth God's role would be in a situation like that. Everyone faces that big *Why* question at some point, but for me it became immediate and necessary to answer. I began a long process of trying to answer that question.

At that point I entered an ambiguous relationship with the Adventist Church because of these big questions I had. I think it took me about five years after my parents' death to gradually pull myself away from the church until I was away from it completely. I had so many links with it—my entire circle of friends, my habits of life, my mom's relatives, the college I attended—everything was oriented to Adventism. So even though I had an enormous faith crisis to deal with, my daily existence was wrapped up in Adventism.

Finally, in 1986, I exited the church. It was at the point where I had to find some answers to my faith questions in a separate environment from the church culture I grew up in. And the only way to do it, it seemed, was to separate myself completely. I didn't know how long it was going to take, or if it would be a permanent state.

What sort of life did you have away from the church community?

I had a rather strange life when I was somewhat in the SDA church community. I was in it because I couldn't seem to get away from it. I didn't have the wherewithal at the age of eighteen and nineteen to up and break ties with everything and everyone I'd ever known.

I went to an Adventist college seven months after my parents died, and at that college, of course, church attendance and religion classes are required. I didn't have a big problem conforming. I wasn't really happy, but it wasn't as difficult for me as for people who didn't have any faith questions. There are people who go to Adventist college, and they just can't deal with being required to attend certain spiritual things, so they leave again. But it wasn't particularly a problem for me, I guess, because I didn't care either way.

But gradually through those five years of attending Adventist college (much of which was paid for by the General Conference), I began to find ways to get around some of the rules, particularly the church attendance one, because that was the one thing that I felt had no meaning to me and was the biggest bother and was not the place where I was getting any answers.

So I used to sign out as though I was going to a church in the surrounding community and then go and do my own thing. I'd go to the library downtown, go to watch movies, study—I did a lot of studying on Saturday mornings in those years. It got to the extreme of studying my history assignment in the back of the balcony of the college church if I couldn't get away, and doing it openly so people wouldn't have any mistake about my attitude toward it.

It was an odd existence, continuing to be around the subculture I'd grown up in with no spiritual reason to be there.

I think pretty soon after I got to that college, even in my first year, I started drinking beer now and then. Never did anything else in terms of drugs. I had never felt any moral compunction to avoid alcohol, so I started drinking. And a lot of times that's what I did for fun with my friends.

It was the kind of thing where I found out that I don't have an addictive personality; fortunately, at least not in that area. So there were only a few times when I drank a lot. Most of the time it was a recreational thing.

When I finished undergraduate college and looked at graduate schools, I went to California to a public university and made an attempt to find myself. I got involved in a couple of clubs on campus and for the first time made a number of friends who were not only not Adventists but didn't consider themselves

Christians. I went to all kinds of concerts in Los Angeles and did a lot of recreation—going to the beach and that kind of thing. I considered my time my own and spent the weekends studying or doing these things I'm talking about.

For those couple of years my life became secular in attitude and practice. I picked up an attitude of what I would now call aggressive defensiveness. At the time I thought it was assertiveness—being protective of yourself and looking out for yourself in all situations in a way I'd never had to do before and also never thought of doing. I think in the end it made me kind of arrogant, but actually I seemed probably quite mild to people in the environment I was in then. Not that I particularly wanted to be rude or inconsiderate to people, but for the first time I was not around the Adventist environment where, at least a lot of the time, you could count on a certain level of goodwill from people. Not that there aren't problems among Adventist people, but they're nothing compared to the unpredictable problems that develop among people who make up their own moral code.

Now, I would be doing those people outside the church a disservice to say that none of them have good qualities. I had several good friends who were very good to me and who had their own good morals. Some of them didn't believe in sleeping around, some didn't believe in doing drugs of any kind. People tended to figure out their own moral code, whatever they thought was right. It wasn't like I was with people who were drifting through life in a state of carnal abandon.

Probably the best thing about that time in my life is that it exposed me to a vast multitude of outlooks on life, and it was then that I began to realize I had really only looked at the world through one point of view for the first twenty-one years of my life. And it wasn't that I had been looking at the world from a God-based point of view all those years, which I think would have been quite adequate, quite broad enough. It was that I had been looking at the world from an Adventist point of view with the Christian element absent. It was woefully inadequate and extremely narrow.

So I discovered people who grew up around a multitude of other Christian points of view, lots of variations amongst those, and then people who had multiple points of view from a non-Christian perspective. If you have grown up as I did—only around Adventists—you cannot begin to imagine the variety of experience people go through. It sounds trite to say this to anyone who has been outside the church or who has not lived a sheltered life in some other way.

Even though I would not say that I found truth where I ended up outside the church, I will say I found a lot of helpful revelation. And I needed it because I needed to know what I did not believe, and I needed some context for what I had grown up with. And this is what I finally got by separating myself from the church for a while.

Did you think about the church in general or your congregation specifically while you were gone?

I did think about the church in the social sense, because even where I was in California, I was only a few miles from some close friends who were still churchgoers. So I would see them and occasionally even end up in church with them. It seemed just a small part of

my world at that time, that I could slip in and out of
without even thinking. To go from there to some reception on campus and drink wine—it was almost seam-
less at the time because I was on this big search and a
lot of the barriers that were there before had come down.
I didn't think about being a part of a congregation, obviously, because that would have defeated the purpose of
separating myself from the culture.

I was aware all through those years that I still had
membership at the church I was baptized into in Africa. And because I had moved quite quickly a couple
of times after I left Africa, first to England, then the
U.S., I think the people at the church in Africa had
lost track of me. It wasn't until after I finished graduate school in California that I even thought of doing
anything about it. Even though I had been gone seven
years, they had not taken my name off the books at
the church in Africa.

So I did sometimes find myself in church in those
years away. One interesting thing is that because I
would sometimes end up at church, I viewed the
people I met there with skepticism, although I didn't
show it.

I think with some of them it was well-placed because I found that, even though there was a lot of
effort by some pastors there to draw people like medi-
cal students and community members to exercise
their Christianity by at least being friendly to people
around them in the church, even at the moments
when they were encouraging this type of thing in the
church service, some people would actively ignore me.

I found it amusing because I wasn't there to be included, and I didn't take offense at it. But I thought it
was so obvious sometimes that it seemed as though they
were trying to get rid of people. So not much was going

on to recommend church to me. And I was not even remotely getting answers to my own faith crisis.

I had read C. S. Lewis's *Mere Christianity* for an undergraduate class and written a paper on it. It had mainly been an intellectual exercise. In fact, I had spent some Saturday mornings at the public library working on the paper. It did straighten out in my mind some of the rationale for being a Christian, mostly the philosophical reasons. But it didn't work for me; it didn't fit. And in that book he wasn't attempting to answer the questions I was asking—how God relates to us and what His role is in catastrophic events.

Did you have any contact with the church while you were gone?

It was strange that I met the girl I ended up marrying while I was in California. She had never heard of Adventists and hadn't gone to church for many of her growing-up years. But when she went to college, she met some girls who invited her to church, and she had gone to a couple different denominations with them, just looking around. So she was exploring that type of thing when I met her.

Sometime after we got to know each other, I took her to church just to see what she'd think. Because I thought, *Well, I really like this girl, but if she's totally a fish out of water in the environment I grew up in, then that may be telling me something.* But she seemed OK with it. It was somewhat like the Baptist surroundings she'd had at church as a small child. So she felt quite at home there, perhaps more than I did.

Our relationship got pretty serious after that. And occasionally we would go to church. It was usually so that I could go and see a friend of mine, and neither of us was particularly leaning toward making it a permanent part of our lives.

So I had this on-off contact, and so did my girl-friend, even though she still didn't know much about Adventists.

When did you first think of returning, and what prompted it?

When I finished grad school, I had a problem. I had been at college in the U.S. on a student visa, and I had to let it run out the summer I finished. I could have continued in the doctoral program for another year or so and then would have had to leave for good. I had run out of years that the INS would renew my visa.

I decided to find a way to stay in the country and see where my relationship with my girlfriend was going. I was aware all the way through college that the only straightforward way for me to immigrate to the U.S. was to get employment with the church, ironically. The church had the legal means to make this changeover from one kind of visa to another.

And because of what had happened to my parents while they were employees of the church, being mur-dered in the mission field (as it was called in those days), there were several General Conference offic-ers who had taken an interest in me and stayed in touch. They had said all along that this visa could be available to me. I was very grateful for this. It cer-tainly gave me a favorable impression of people high up in the church hierarchy, that they didn't ignore the plight of people lower down.

I began to look around at things like academy teach-ing jobs. Nothing became evident in that area. I sent out résumés, made some phone calls, and did make some attempt to get a position. Then I switched to plan B and contacted both publishing houses, thinking I could possibly get in on the ground floor at one of those. After talking to someone at each publisher, the person I talked to suggested I send in a résumé so they could find me if something came up.

At that point I was getting half-hearted about the whole exercise, and I didn't send the résumés. So I was looking at leaving the country. I really didn't consider getting married so I could stay. I didn't think that was an appropriate option.

Out of the blue I got a phone call from one of the General Conference people who had stayed in touch, and he said that Pacific Press was trying to find me and that they had a job opening. They had not heard anything from me. So I thought, *Great, I'll talk to the guy*. The VP actually came to my apartment for an interview. Pretty soon after that, apparently on the recommendation of the person at the GC, I was hired at Pacific Press.

Lest anyone think this was a bad reflection on how Pacific Press conducted business, I will say that they were very careful. I didn't lie to them about anything, but they mostly directed their questions about whether I would be an acceptable employee to the individual at the General Conference, and, as far as I know, hired me on his word.

As I look back, I see evidence of Providence working in my life through those years. I think there were indications much earlier in my life, but I didn't see them.

I took the job at Pacific Press with the intention of immediately beginning this process of changing to a permanent visa to stay in the U.S. I decided I would give the job long enough to get through this and then work a little longer to pay my dues and then take off and do what I wanted to do, which was to work for a secular book publisher. I'd actually been lined up to take a summer course in editing and book publishing when I got the call from Pacific Press.

So I moved to Idaho sight unseen, just loaded up my stuff in a U-Haul, and showed up there, found an apartment and began working as a proofreader to begin with. And then moved on to copy editing.

At that point it became necessary to appear to be Adventist somewhat. That was not appealing to me whatsoever. I was hooked on a secular lifestyle, watching TV on Friday nights to wind down, drinking a little here and there, going to a bar now and then to hang out.

I realized I could jeopardize my plans by being careless and decided I would have to shape up and just deal with it for a while. I had grown up doing all the Adventist things, so it was sort of like putting on a coat to go back to acting like one, regardless of my actual spiritual state.

So that's what I did. I quit drinking permanently, which was not a difficult thing. Not that I did it willingly, but it wasn't difficult once I decided it was what I should do.

I began to visit the churches to decide which one I could stand to go to all the time and decided on the church downtown. So I became a regular attender again, although I had no thought of getting involved. I thought it was kind of a perfect situation that I would show up at this church every week and avoid people, and I don't know how many times the greeter asked me if I was a visitor, and this would be months after I had started attending. I thought things were going well if they still thought I was a visitor.

The key here is that I had to proofread the books

Pacific Press was putting out. As soon as I got into working there, I was reading at least one, sometimes two books a day. I'd proofread a 96-page book in a morning. Later I became a copy editor for these books and worked on a more intimate level with the manuscripts, checking Bible and Ellen White quotes, checking sources, and looking for grammar problems.

So I became really wrapped up in these products, and I read several personal-story type books, a couple of which were very intense stories about someone's very difficult life and their ultimate deliverance from these difficulties. I also read a Morris Venden book each year and Clifford Goldstein's books. Coming from a very secular master's program and secular environment, absent of any spiritual influence, I only wanted to improve the technical quality of these books somewhat. That was my only concern then—to do the job right.

I had only been there a few months when these products began to have an effect on me. I began to understand what is high priority in the Christian life and what is not. Not that the practices of our religion, our particular subculture, are not important, but I got some perspective on them.

I read the writings of people who I consider really understand the ministry of Jesus and His basic message, and also some of the primary principles of God's order of things. My mind filled up with these things almost by default. I couldn't keep them out, because it was my job.

I worked on getting that employment visa for eleven months. I went through a lot of money traveling to Canada twice and then back to England, trying to get an INS official to approve a work visa for me.

Again I'd have to say I can look back and see all kinds of workings of Providence. If I had been aware of it at the time, I think I would have been greatly disturbed by that idea. But I didn't notice. So it just seemed I was going through great difficulty with the visa and I would just hang on until I got through it, and then when it was done I would go off and do my thing.

Well, after the eleven months my girlfriend was wondering if I would ever make up my mind whether we were going to get married and settle down or if I was going to do something else. It had been a year since I moved, and she had recently moved to Idaho too. We were considering where our lives should go, and I was beginning to feel the effects of this material that I had to work on every day.

Not that it changed my life in practice at first. Probably for a couple of years after I worked for Pacific Press, I still didn't particularly care about what happened on a Saturday afternoon or a Friday night nor what I ate nor about a lot of the lifestyle guidelines Adventists follow. And I was almost purposely avoiding dealing with them, because I had grown up with them, and I thought, if I go back to some of the more superficial things, I'm never going to make any headway with the big questions I have.

The perspective I was gaining on what the Christian life means was beginning to give me the basic answer I was looking for as to what God's role is in the universe, particularly in our messed-up part of it.

How long did it take before you considered yourself a full member again?

That's a hard thing to pinpoint. I've not been re-baptized. I can't specify a time when I can say I returned to God, although there's definitely a time period in the first six months I lived in Idaho and worked at Pacific Press where my heart and my way of looking at things began to change direction almost unconsciously. I think if I had thought about it much at the beginning, I would have resisted it a lot.

I would have to say the Holy Spirit was talking to me, and I was not shutting Him out. I began to sense that I was onto something good, and I couldn't explain what or why. I wasn't going to fight feeling better about my life, and I wasn't going to reject something that seemed to promise better things in the future. So I would say it took about three years to reach the point where I had settled a lot of the bigger questions, and I was able to turn my attention to some of the more practical aspects of life—whether I was going to rent Woody Allen movies on Friday night or not or do grocery shopping on Saturday afternoon—these kinds of things were not my concern during the first couple of years of reemerging faith. And I thought, all in good time, as long as I'm not a stumbling block to anyone who's in the church or who might think they'd have to fire me from my job if they saw me doing any of this. I pretty much stayed away from that much controversy.

So it was probably three years into my work that I felt I had completely returned to God and to the church I grew up in.

What was it like actually returning to church?

I had plenty of practice before I did it for real. I do think I got a good perspective of the church from coming back in the way I did though. Some of the problems you encounter in a church did not concern me, didn't worry me. It didn't concern me whether people were friendly or not, whether they were fighting among themselves or at peace, or if people seemed materialistic or seemed to be nominal Adventists or

nominal Christians. It didn't even particularly concern me when people were hypocritical, although that
does bother me now, because I think it's so detrimen-
tal to the advancement of God's cause. At the time I
was coming back to the church, I didn't feel that I
was above those things so much as they didn't concern me. Those problems were outside my personal
experience of church.

My time of becoming active in the church again coin-
cided with my meeting some young people who were
also gradually coming into a time of church activity
themselves. We began the process of growing a young-
adult group that became very active after a couple of
years. Almost from day one we called it the Salt Company. It took a long time and a lot of steps. I know I
grew a lot, along with some of the others in the group,
so the later times of my stronger faith and active par-
ticipation are tied with the growth of that group.

Did you run into problems returning to the church?

I don't think I've had problems since I came back.
I've *seen* a lot of problems in the six years I've been par-
ticipating in church again. Examples of the types of problems that drive people out: I've had people be border-
line rude to me and kind of unwelcoming. I've seen some
indifference and materialistic preoccupation and all the
rest of it—leadership crises and so on.

But I have to say again that these things are not
particularly my concern. And I think this is because
I understand the church in the sense of it being God's
children, that God knows His children and they know
Him, because they hear His voice. And even though I
can't be the one to tell who those people are and who
amongst the church members are not, I still have the

assurance that the flock exists because God has said so. I'm anxious and happy to be part of that flock.

I didn't run into problems with the lifestyle in this church. I was used to it. I never really had disagreements with the main things. That's not what made me leave. They were the kind of things I didn't follow when I didn't want to and did when I wanted to. Ever since I've gained that basic understanding of what it means to be a follower of God, those habits of life and guidelines of behavior have seemed quite acceptable and actually quite rational.

Have you learned anything valuable from the way your life unfolded?

I've learned things in several areas. I've learned a new understanding of what is most important in life. And that is what Jesus said is the most important commandment.

Now when He called it a commandment, I've come to understand, that's a term He gave as an indicator of God's order of things. Because we are God's created beings, it's perfectly natural for us to love Him. And if we were back in our perfect state, we *would* love Him with all our hearts and all our minds and all our souls. If we were perfect in Him, we would also love our neighbors the same way we love ourselves (or should love ourselves).

This to me is very desirable. It wasn't until I understood how desirable it is that the whole Christian life made any sense to me. That was my first step in understanding and was the most important one I had to reach.

Beyond that, I've come to understand some things about how God is involved in our lives, whether it's in catastrophe or in our day-to-day living. I under-

stand that God's protection is, first of all, spiritual.
When we think about the promise that He will send
His angels to keep us from dashing our foot against a
stone, He is talking about the physical life to the extent that He likewise has concern for the sparrows. I
agree that He does. But that doesn't mean that sparrows don't die in this world. And people die too.

So I understand His protection from the point of
view of when Peter talks about the roaring lion seeking whom he may devour. God's protection is prom-
ised in that we will not lose our souls even if we lose
our physical lives. And that to me is our highest priority. There's no point in becoming a Christian if you
don't understand that ultimate goal, that greatest
goal, which is to spend eternity with God.

Even though my parents died a violent death, one
that makes me uncomfortable to this day, I had to learn
after all those years to distinguish between the fact that
they felt great pain at the time (and I felt great pain
afterward) and the fact that God wants to do away with
pain of all kinds—the kind of physical and mental torture we feel on earth. To mix up the two ideas and say
that somehow God's ultimate purpose is compromised
by the pain that people suffer on earth is a mistake.
They're really two separate things.

This is not to say that we should not claim the promise of God for happiness at all or for protection when
we're doing His work. But we quickly forget the pref-
ace to any request for protection and that is, Thy will
be done. Really, that's the prayer you could pray any
time when you do anything that would put you in
harmony with God. If you never prayed for protection again for a road trip, I would say if you place
yourself in harmony with the will of God and in sub-
mission to the will of God, He is able and willing to

protect you according to the way He thinks is right.

That was a big step for me, understanding where the tragic end of my parents fitted in with the cosmic order of things. I would never have been able to come to that understanding without first understanding who God is. God is not only all powerful; He is all good. He is the only thing that is completely good. The opposite of Him is absurd, irrational evil. There is nothing tainted about God. He only wants what is good; He only wants what is good for me.

Once I understood that, then I was able to separate Him from the issue of what happened to my parents.

I'm going into my own opinions here, but I consider that my parents being murdered while they were teachers in Africa was one of those times when the devil won a small battle, but he didn't come any closer to winning his war. I don't know how much understanding the devil has of how the war is going and where it's going to end up. But he seems intent on winning as many little battles as he can, and an awful lot of people are suffering because of it.

The question remained in my mind, Why does God allow this to continue? To tell the truth, I don't really have an answer for that. The reason I don't is that I don't know the details of God's timing. But I think I understand God's sense of timing better than I used to. I know now that He works out His will in people's lives in many different sets of steps, at a different pace for each person. Some experience very sudden changes from the prompting of the Holy Spirit, and some experience it over a long time—that's what happened to me.

This is why I see a big danger in judging, say, people who have withdrawn from the church, because you don't know whether they will listen to the voice of God in the future. And if they do, you don't know

which way God will lead them. So when you find someone who is half-way back to Him and treat them as
an outcast or total sinner, you're pretty much destroy-
ing the handiwork of God.

What else have you learned?

I've learned that my life goes to pieces very quickly
when I stop submitting myself to God. I've made a
couple of big decisions in the last few years without
God and regretted them afterward. It's strange that
it seems almost guaranteed to fail without Him. I
think the reason is that God wants me to stay aware
of how much I depend on Him from day to day. Also,
He wants me to be aware of what the devil would
like to do if he could get a hand in.

This doesn't mean I don't experience trials anymore,
because I do. I understand the place of those now, that
they are not only to test me, but I understand now how
many things that have happened in my life are a parallel of what happened to Job. I prove God to be right by
keeping faithful to Him no matter what happens. And
that means sometimes there are great difficulties, great
challenges, that could tear down my faith, which re-
quire me to again look at what our ultimate goal is and
again look to the object of our goal—God Himself.

Do you have any regrets?

I really don't. I can't think of any.

**What are your goals now that you're back in
the church?**

I now understand in a way I didn't in the first twenty-
five years of my life how one's life unfolds with God as a
step-by-step process. Each step is exciting to me. Now
and then I feel I'm going a step forward and a couple of

steps back. But I realize that's because I cannot expect that in this life I'll go up and up and up.

So my goal is to continue growing. I want to continue to allow God to teach me what He wants me to know so I'll mature over time and I can use the gifts He's given me more effectively and understand how to use them better.

I also want to become more dependent on Him to show me where I'm needed in His work and not to think I just have to take that burden on myself, that I have to be the one to force myself to get out and take part.

Probably the fundamental change in approach I've had to Seventh-day Adventism is that to me it's no longer a religion of what I ought to do or what I absolutely should do; it's now a religion of what I want to do. And that is, I want to follow God and want to do what He says is the best thing to do. So there aren't any "oughts" in my life. I don't go to church on Sabbath because I ought to. I don't keep a healthy body because I ought to. I don't share my faith because I ought to. These are all things I do because I want to. And I don't do them just because I have to for God but because I want to do them. I have a sense of gratitude toward God that He has made His way this way, because the way He wants us to live is all positive.

I believe He can show me the way to contribute to the work that needs to be done on this earth, inside or outside the church. I work for the denomination right now. I don't work for the denomination because I think I ought to; I now work for the denomination because God has led me to a particular job. I would say He almost gave it to me, which is very gratifying because it's not a job I feel I can take credit for, and yet I find it very enjoyable.

What would you say to those who have left the church and who currently have no intention of returning?

I'm not much of a talker, so I probably wouldn't have much to say to them. But if they had any questions, well, let's say they didn't. Let's say they simply had no interest in the church. If the opportunity arose in a conversation, I think I would tell them that God has His own agenda and His own pace for doing things, His own timing. I would suggest that they keep an open mind about His leading and not think particularly whether He's pointing them toward any church or the Adventist Church. Those kinds of steps in one's life come when it's appropriate, when God sees fit.

I would say to them that God is still very much interested in them. It would depend on the individual, but if I could discover their attitude toward God, I would talk about God. I know there are people who have a very bad attitude about God Himself, never mind the church. So I might tell about some of the good things I've discovered about God, that basically everything about God is good.

If they had concerns about the Adventist Church, I would say to them, Go back and deal with your relationship with God first. Don't try to resolve problems you had with the church before you are straight with God.

To people who feel they have a good relationship with God but have a complaint about the church, I would probably only say that I hope they would continue to open themselves to God's leading and that if God wants them back in the church that they would let Him lead them. Perhaps I wouldn't say that. But I would suggest they keep their minds open to God.

What would you say to lifelong members?

I'm not sure how well you can become convinced of this without experiencing it in your own life, but I would urge lifelong members to observe how God works over long periods of time in the lives of others. And I would ask them to accept the idea that there are some people who may be a bit shaky on some of the external things but it's impossible to judge their spiritual condition from these things. So it would be presumptuous to treat people as though we know what's right for them because of what we've observed.

This is not to condone open sin, but people who are intentionally sinning—I think that attitude is not difficult to discern. Such people give themselves away by their attitude. But there are so many people on the fringes of the church who are searching and wanting to find their way in, whose intentions are good. I think we need to do much more to encourage them, without condoning anything that is harmful or immoral.

This is a perspective I've been given for a reason, I believe. I haven't had to exercise it very much, but it's something I'd encourage lifelong members to think about.

What's your advice to new converts?

Be prepared for the times that the only thing that will keep your faith intact is to look at Jesus and what He is like. I would warn them that any church, Adventist or other, is filled with human beings who have not reached perfection. Trials in the way you relate to the church *will* arise. You will have to deal with faith crises.

So I'd suggest they be prepared, and the only way to get through these times is to keep your eyes on Jesus. I realize that doesn't necessarily tell them how to keep their connection with the Adventist Church strong. But again I would say that, seeing how people's lives go through steps, I believe God's purposes are achieved in the lives of people who are open to Him even when we can't tell whether they have a solid connection to the church or not.

In conclusion, I would say the Bible has turned out to be the best resource for feeding my faith. I have had a continuous pleasure in reading the Bible since those days a few years ago when my perspective on God and the Christian life became real to me.

It doesn't cease to amaze me how, when my mind is open to God's guidance, so many of the life experiences recorded in the Bible make good parallels to my life. Sure, there's a huge culture gap and chronological gap there—several thousand years from the earliest events in the Bible. And yet it's so obvious that the human characteristics of those people are so similar to mine, to ours. Some of the things we do, the traps we fall into, the cycles of life that are played out in Bible stories, are so similar to what we deal with now. It tends to be the details that are different.

I've gotten a lot of insight from comparing the kind of theocratic society Jesus lived in with the church culture I grew up in. It's been helpful for me to get some of my attitudes from the way Jesus acted in His day. Not to say I'm looking at our leadership as Pharisees. That's absolutely the wrong parallel here. But to keep in mind the sense that Jesus, when He spoke to people around Him, knew what and how much to assume because of their common religious background, and that's the screen through which I see a lot of the things He says in the Gospels.

When I consider how much of a burden I have for unbelievers, particularly people in my extended family, I have to think about how Jesus went beyond the society He grew up in to relate to people outside of it. The attitudes He displayed and approaches He used seem very useful to me.

I'd have to say that God Himself drew me back with this grand scheme of His, where He got me stuck in a job in which the literature of the church drew me back to Him.

Questions

1. Should pastors be expected to conduct grief therapy? If not, who should take the role in the church?

2. Has there been a generation (or two) in the Adventist Church that missed the love of God in their own lives and therefore missed His joy?

3. Should we stop young people from being baptized if we perceive they know and accept the truth but have not met God personally (have no testimony)?

4. Christian martyrdom is happening in countries outside North America. What will our reaction be if it begins to happen in the United States?

5. As a church we still evangelize through print, but we do very little to reach the MTV generations through the media they use—video and video games, movies, music, television, the Internet. How can we reach these people groups? Can we afford to? Can we afford not to? Who should start?

Chapter 7

Cindy

---

early forties, wife of Mike (see chapter 8), mother, homemaker

---

Tell me about your earliest experience with the Seventh-day Adventist Church.

My uncle and aunt and cousins were Adventists. But I didn't know anything about what being a Christian was or anything. All I knew was they didn't eat meat and they were nice people. We saw them like once a year. And that's all I knew until I was in eighth grade.

Then a Baptist group that I was going with, with our neighbors, were meeting in an Adventist church that Mike and I later became members of. It was interesting that we started going to church in that building; it was unreal. And later I thought, *God's work is so wonderful*. It was in that church I gave my heart to Jesus, when I was thirteen, as a Baptist in the Adventist church building.

Other than that, I didn't have any contact with the Adventist Church until 1983, when I met an Adventist lady in another Baptist church I was going to. She worked in the nursery. She was just a wonderful lady, so gracious, I thought.

So she was the one who changed your mind on some things?

Well, I didn't really know anything about Adventists at all. Nothing negative. The only thing I knew was they were vegetarians. I had become an almost total vegetarian. At least, I thought. I still ate some fish sometimes and chicken, but I was very health-conscious. And God was really teaching me that my body is the temple of God's Holy Spirit.

This lady and I both ended up at the grocery store after Sunday service one day. We both said something about making our own bread as we were purchasing a loaf of bread. Both of us muttered, "Oh, I usually make my own." I said, "You usually make your own?" Because I didn't know anyone else who made their own bread on a regular basis as I did. And she said, "Yes, in fact, most of our church as a whole, we're very health-minded, and we make everything from scratch."

So I was very interested in that, and so we got to visiting, and that very day she invited me to go to a Revelation seminar and a film series at her church. So she came and picked me up, me and my three little children. Mike was at work. I went three nights that week. It was wonderful; I loved it. And at the end of the week she gave me a booklet on the mark of the beast. I read it, and I knew it was truth.

So I never went back to the Sunday church. I just called my pastor; I went over to visit him. I called several of my friends and told them about the Sabbath, and a couple of them accepted the Sabbath. My

Baptist preacher told me I was going to hell, and my husband would never be saved.

It was really exciting to join the true church.

So that was another stage in your experience—you'd been converted, and this was another step?

Yes, because all of a sudden I saw that God said to worship on the seventh day, and I hadn't been doing it. I'd been doing it on the first day, and I thought, *Well, that makes sense.* So that was no problem.

That lady sat down that same week in my house, before she gave me the booklet on the mark of the beast, and she kind of walked me through some things in the Bible first. She showed the state of the dead, how people didn't go straight up to heaven, and how they go to sleep until Jesus comes. She showed me several things, and I just thought it was so wonderful to find out these truths.

So I started taking my different versions of the Bible—I think I had four at the time—and I was just studying madly. I was also reading Jehovah's Witnesses material, Mormon material, and I had prayed about it all. And I felt very secure in the idea that God will guide us, through His Holy Spirit, into all truth.

So after that, you became more familiar with what it was like to be around Adventists?

Eight months after I first went to the Adventist Church, my husband was baptized, and I joined the church by profession of faith. We had just moved, so we went back to the little church where we had been going before to be baptized. We had an elderly pastor, and Mike loved him so much he had him baptize him. We knew all the people back there, and we'd only been going a couple weeks to the church at our new home.

I remember going to that new, larger church and thinking, *I don't think I'm in an Adventist church*. Because I equated an Adventist church with ladies who didn't wear makeup and jewelry—and I had just given up all my makeup and my pierced ears and my long fingernails and my rings and necklaces. I gave everything away. Nobody told me to. I wanted to, and I didn't think I was trying to earn anything. It made very good sense to me that I would be adorned in a natural way and that I'd be better off without it, and I'd be a better witness, and I could spend my money better elsewhere. I'd be adorned in heaven with those kinds of things. I just wanted to be very simple in appearance.

So when I went to the Adventist Church in a larger city and saw all these ladies all decked out, I was really surprised. I remember that no one but two ladies even spoke with me the first couple of times I went. They became very dear friends.

We were going to some evangelistic meetings there, and the one who's still a dear friend, said, "Cindy, keep your eyes on Jesus. Don't look at the people. There's going to be so many doing this and doing that, different things. But don't look at people." And that's what has carried me through the years, that comment she made back in 1983.

I was really upset. Why weren't these Adventist ladies following the truth?

Did you feel uncomfortable with those things all along before you went away from the church?

I have always been active in a conference church all through the years. But I was always open to meetings and things that sounded interesting. You know, I thought if I can learn something, I'll go and I'll glean.

But what did happen is that we started getting a newsletter, and it was pretty legalistic, more focused on works than on a relationship with Jesus. With my personality, totally opposite to Mike's, I thought, *Boy, anything I can do to be closer to God, or to make God happy, I'll do it.* It was more of a concentration on things I was doing instead of letting Him do things in me. You know, trying too hard.

So through that publication we were drawn more and more to fringe things. We did get involved with a lot of the people who thought that way. So I did get quite rigid in many areas. But I still went to an SDA church. Some of them thought I was off my rocker, I'm sure, when I only wore tights and wouldn't wear nylons.

Sometimes I would get upset at some of the things I would see. Not at the church in general, but some of the things happening in the church. I wrote a letter to the union paper back in about 1987. I told them I wasn't going to leave the Adventist Church unless they booted me out, but I felt that we needed higher standards and we needed to be obedient. They printed my letter.

I really focused on obedience, which I still think is very important, but it was a cramped obedience. Not a joyful obedience as I experience now. I still am obedient and love to hold high standards, but for a different reason. Not trying to impress anybody or please this crowd or that crowd. I don't care what people think anymore, I only want to please the Lord.

So was there a definite period when you felt this way and put yourself at a distance from certain types of Adventists?

Yes, there was. And I think that was very judgmental of me. Many of these folk don't realize that's where they're coming from. Somehow, you set yourself up as a little bit better. I didn't think that I thought that way at the time, but looking back you can see more than when you're right in the midst of something.

I was just trying to do what I thought was right. But I thought I needed to make everyone else do it too. We can't do that. I didn't realize then that you cannot coerce anyone into doing anything. You have to live it yourself, and they choose to do it that way, too, or if they don't, then that's their business.

As far as the church itself, the structure and some of the policies and things are concerned, I would get some publications that told different things we were doing with our money and doing with church decisions. I always read them with an open mind and didn't believe everything I read. I figured that some of it might be true and some of it might not be.

Eventually, after Mike and I had a real difficult time between the two of us, when I was so rigid and legalistic and he was so loose, I didn't want any of those publications anymore. I wrote them all and asked them not to send their stuff to me. I was just going to read the Bible and the Spirit of Prophecy and a few things from authors who I felt had balance and true love for God and others.

I think the thing that occurs is that everyone is so focused on loving God, but part of loving God is loving each other. We forget that. It gets out of balance.

Did your life change after you had strict standards? What did it involve?

In some areas. I went back to wearing jeans and slacks, besides dresses. I still like dresses and jumpers and wear them a lot. I still am modest.

Before, I was at a time when because of the people I was associating with and the things I was reading, I felt I couldn't wear any pants at all. When I changed, I went back to wearing shorts—not short shorts, mind you. But I did shift.

I've seen a lot of friends who went through this, because I've been observing this through the years, and I didn't shoot back over as far, and I don't know why. I never went back to makeup or jewelry or anything where you look made up.

As far as inward things, I became more relaxed and more accepting of others. And through the years, that's just grown. I guess it's been about six or seven years since all that occurred.

I've had my hard times this last year too. Not to do with the church as a whole. I started going to an offshoot group instead of to the local church, only because they were very loving people. The church I was attending at the time, it's a different church because it's the kind of place that has a lot of visitors, where you never see the same person twice. There's a very small nucleus of people who are regulars because this is a tourist place.

I was gone for eight months, but I wasn't against the church at all. I even told them that; it wasn't doctrinal or anything. I talked to the head elder, who I'm good friends with, and told him I didn't have anyone whom I could really relate to in the church. Nobody had teenagers except for two other families, and they were in a whole different mind-set than I was. They were in super-loose-land, and I was over in trying to train up these children for Jesus.

So that's why we went away for a little while. Now the kids are at an Adventist academy, I'm back to the old church, and am doing fine. I still kept relationships there during that time.

And this offshoot group, they're really neat people. But they kept splitting hairs. If they want to split them on their own, fine. But to say that everyone is preaching error and all this stuff, I don't think that's true.

What led you to the offshoot group?

I had been in a car accident, and I needed some nurturing. I felt as if I wasn't getting any. When you work in that capacity yourself, you don't get calls, you don't get cards or notes or letters.

I've been trying to remember that. It's made me very sensitive to be careful of the ones who are the workers, the nucleus of the church—when they're not there, writing them a note or calling them, saying, "Hey, I missed you last week." I've always done that kind of stuff for new people, for people who were teetering or looked like they needed a little lifting. Or maybe my close buddies. But I think there are many who don't get reached out to.

After that car accident, I didn't come to church for several weeks. And then I came, and it was very hard for me to sit. I'd broken my sternum and had a lot of bruising and had had a concussion. I had gotten some calls the first two days, Mike had said. I couldn't really do anything, but later I lay in bed and wrote notes to everyone he said had called, thanking them for their concern. After that I never heard anything from anybody, I never got a pastoral visit, and no one visited me except for one girlfriend.

Months went by, and I thought, *Boy, if somebody like me can slip through the cracks . . .* I had a high profile in my congregation.

That's when I went off searching for maybe some deeper friendships, I hoped.

So even if you put a lot of yourself into a church, it's not necessarily reciprocated.

That's right, and it taught me a beautiful lesson.

You see, that's what I was looking for. I was looking for some appreciation, some reciprocation. After the car accident, I didn't drive for about three months. I just kind of stayed home and vegetated. But I started reaching out, because I knew enough that I would really be in bad shape if I didn't. So I wrote those notes.

I heard that the pastor's wife had smashed her finger and cut it open in the garage door and had to get stitches and stuff. So I wrote her a little note, and I remember my feelings at the time. Weeks and months went by, and I didn't think of anything right away. I didn't expect a quick response, but I did expect one eventually. But it never came. And I was really hurt by that. Very hurt.

For months I kind of wallowed in these little hurts, feeling like nobody really cared about me. Finally, earlier this year, I realized that Jesus cares. You know, people are so busy, and they don't mean to inflict any hurt at all. There were some who attacked me, but they were the exceptions, not the rule.

But I decided my reputation belonged to the Lord. I wasn't going to care what anybody did to me. I was sailing high in the Lord, and then all that stuff happened. And I felt like, oh, boy, here's another test, and this one's the bigger one. And I finally got through it this last spring.

But it is a blessing if we can look at all those hurts and realize they are just wonderful educational tools, to be able to know what not to do to others! It's not fun to be forgotten, to be neglected.

Even though people attacked you, that's not what drove you away.

Not at all. I never did have that happen. Mike kind of did. He had some really terrible experiences. When he was on the board of a health food concern, because he still ate cheese, they decided to write him off. I was quite angry in my heart about that, but I knew they were just people. They shouldn't have done that; it wasn't right. And it wasn't the church. It was some people.

But that comment from years ago kept me going, that it was problem people and not the church. I never equated the two. When I think of the church, I think of God's faithful people. And the ones that hurt, I would think in my mind, are God's unfaithful people.

Are there any areas of belief in the church that you had difficulty with?

Yes. Just one area. The 1844 investigative judgment. It seems to make sense that that's what occurred, that Jesus went into the Most Holy Place at that time. It could be. But I don't like to put a lot of emphasis on anything like that, only because I don't think it has a lot of relevance right now.

Maybe I'm way off, but in my life as a Christian, I don't see a lot of help in that area; I don't see how it draws me closer to Christ. And I don't know how it would help me help someone else to bring them into a closer relationship with the Lord. We know that we all have to be accountable for ourselves, but we've got the passages of Scripture, you know, "Be ye also ready: for in such an hour as ye think not the Son of man cometh."

And another thing I don't like dwelling on is "historic" Adventism. That's probably what turned me off about the little group I was going to. They decided to call themselves "historic" Adventists. I think it's corny. I mean, we're all part of history, and I love history. But I think if you stay in the past, you cannot make any progress in the present.

I believe that too many people follow it because they think it's the thing to do, because it's popular in these circles. It's the "in" thing to do, to be in the know about our Adventist past.

More important is, What is Christ doing right now? And in our own past, how God has led us, how He has taught us and shown us His wonderful grace. And in Scripture, the things that happened in the past that have so many wonderful lessons for us.

When you and Mike were at odds over his spiritual state, did you feel pulled one way by your beliefs and pulled the other by him?

I don't know that I felt pulled any way at all. I just thought that he was in the wrong and I was right. I thought I was being faithful and he wasn't. The focus was on what he wasn't doing.

I didn't relate a loving picture of the Lord all the time. I thought I did. But I was always giving him little stabs, and all I could see were the outward things I was doing for him and putting up with. I didn't realize the little looks we give, the little comments.

Are you happy being back with the church you go to?

Yes, that hurtful church that I now love! But I still love those other [offshoot] people, too, and I still fellowship with them a little, although I don't go to the service. On Wednesday nights sometimes I'll get together with them for their studies on Daniel and other things in the Bible. I haven't thought, *Oh, you dirty, rotten sinners; I don't want to have anything to do with you, because I'm going back to the conference church.* They know why I went back. I told them I felt I could be used more there, and I decided to overcome the bitterness I had in my heart and forgive. So they know why I stopped fellowshiping with them.

Do you have some goals now?

I would like to help others be more accepting of each other and to have a better understanding of what it means to love each other as Jesus wants us to, so we will be known by our love.

I pray for more opportunities to help others understand where some of those people in the fringe groups are coming from, to bridge the gap. That's what I'd like to see, because I see most of those people in the fringe groups as people who have been hurt. So they have formed their own little group.

Some in the church get hurt and do what I did. They form an offshoot group and think, *We're gonna play church, and we're gonna be as good as we can be. We're gonna do everything right.* And then there's that other group; they don't go and form a church. They go back home, and they go back into the ways they had before, the ways of the world. They say, Why bother?

I think both groups need to see the light of the gospel, that Jesus' love can heal all hurts. You don't need to go either way, too far to the left, too far to the right. Just stay in the path of the Lord, and He'll help us to love others.

One of my main goals is to set people free in the area of health. I teach nutrition classes and cooking classes. I have quite a lot of interested people who are non-Adventists from my home school group.

I find it challenging and fun. It's challenging in the church now, because many think it's legalistic to be health-minded, and I'm trying to help dispel that. No, we can't earn our way to heaven by eating right. But we sure can take better care of our bodies and be healthy servants of the Lord.

Questions

1. Are standards of outward appearance a sure sign of inward spiritual condition?

2. Does God eventually lead all individuals to the same standards of lifestyle if they allow Him to, or does He leave room for choices?

3. Is there any merit in the complaints of offshoot groups that the church as a whole has lowered its standards?

4. Should the church attempt to define appropriate, contemporary guidelines, based on the Scriptures, to raise children and teenagers?

5. How do you answer the accusation that the church should be holier than it is?

Chapter 8

Mike

**forties, married to Cindy,
concrete tester**

In your teenage years, did you have much religious experience?

None at all, really, from the home. From when I was ten or eleven, for a few years we went to a community church with a friend of my mom's. And it was not a real good experience, because I wore hand-me-down shoes and my feet always hurt on Sunday. It was a real small church. It was more of a pain to go than anything. I didn't get anything out of it.

The only Christian experience I had from then until I graduated from high school was a Christian history teacher at my school, who had a very profound effect on my life. I don't think he knew it, and I never told him, although I've always wanted to get in touch with him and tell him that he did. And in not so much a relationship with Jesus, but just basic principles of honesty and integrity. What Christians stood for, he showed that in his life, in the classroom. Without preaching.

So that was just in high school?

Yes. Cindy and I met when I was a sophomore and she was a junior. We were drinkers and pot smokers, I guess what you'd call hell-raisers. For me that went on until I found the Lord at twenty-three or twenty-four.

Almost the first time we went to a church was when we got married. I think we went once or twice with Cindy's grandmother and mother at Christmas. That was pretty much the extent of it. That wasn't a religious experience, more of a family commitment.

How did your conversion happen?

Before I found the Lord, Cindy said one day, "I need to start going to church." She started going to a Lutheran church. We had been married a couple years; our first son was just born. She woke up one Sunday and said, "I've got to go to church." I said, "OK, see you later."

She went there six months or so, and she wasn't being fed. I started going fishing with the pastor at the Lutheran church, and he smoked and drank. That was fine with me.

I had hound dogs at the time, and I was looking to get one of my females bred. I talked to a guy and was planning to go over to his house. And he said, "Hey, bring your wife along." I thought, *That's kind of weird*, but I brought her along. The wives got to talking, and the lady invited Cindy to the Baptist church.

She started going. This whole time she was having two or three Bibles out at night, going through different scriptures. At that time her conversion had started. I'd say she was converted in the Baptist church. I was still smoking and drinking and doing what pleases the world and pleased me.

Before Cindy went to church, she had become a

vegetarian. I just went along with the flow. I just thought it was kind of humorous that she'd go to church. But I still loved her, and we still got along. But I was pretty much a pagan.

She went to that church for maybe a year. An Adventist lady was baby-sitting in the Baptist nursery. They started chumming around because they had the health message in common. Then Cindy started going to the Adventist church, and I can remember my heart being pinged and panged a few times about some of the things she would tell me.

The thing that really converted me, I suppose, was going to an evangelistic series by the evangelist in our conference. The night I went, it was on America in prophecy and the mark of the beast. Boy, this guy had me sitting on the edge of my chair. My Christian history teacher had hit on a few things about the Catholic Church, not in a derogatory way, but just the facts. And I thought, *Hey, this evangelist knows what he's talking about.* He really had me fired up.

I think at that point my heart was open enough that the time was right. Although I didn't give my heart to the Lord that night, that was when I was hooked.

So when Cindy talked about things she had heard from Adventists, it didn't shock you?

It did, but at that point in my life I was a rebel without a cause. I needed something that wasn't mediocre. And then when I heard the evangelist speak, it all made sense. It put things together in my heart, and I was ripe, ready to be picked. The Lord's timing is perfect.

During that first period in the Adventist Church, what was your experience?

Well, one time I was over at the house of that lady

who got Cindy interested in Adventism, helping her work on her car. She was a single mother and had several kids, and I was helping her out. The local pastor and that evangelist came over there while I was working and talked to me. And it was the first time I'd had a man of God, or a pastor, actually look me in the eye, give me a firm handshake, and be interested in me. Most of the time before, it was, you know, can't wait to get out of church and have a smoke or a glass of wine. All the other ones in the Sunday churches seemed to be too busy. But these guys actually looked me in the eye, and I could tell they were sincere. And it made a big difference.

And there was an older lady at the local church who wasn't very well off, but every new couple that came into the church, she gave them a hardback Conflict of the Ages series as a gift. I started reading it from the beginning, all the way through, and I just couldn't believe what I was reading. I mean, it got me on fire. The books are what really converted me. I'd go through them with the Bible, and especially when I got into *The Great Controversy*, I found myself rereading chapters completely to get the gist of it. That was when we were really on fire, basically unshakable.

But we were very immature, and we went to another church, a big church, when we moved. Some of the people wore jewelry and makeup and stuff. And Cindy had given all that stuff up on her own, without anybody telling her.

Now, at this point in my life when I see an Adventist woman with makeup or jewelry, I don't look at that stuff; I look at the person. And that's the main difference.

For me, back then, I thought, *why the difference between the small, conservative church and the big one?* But that's where the devil was wanting to tie me up and get me looking, with my eyes off God. So we were at the big city church for three and a half years, and then we went back to the small conservative church.

How far away did you go from the church and for how long?

The small church was right in the middle of a split, or starting to. That's when the camps divided, and sad to say, we got caught up on the wrong side. Cindy didn't quit going to church, but I did.

I started hanging out with the wrong crowd in the church, and the criticism started and the bitterness and the bickering. Before you knew it, I wasn't getting anything out of church, and my focus had completely switched. The bitterness took over, the devil got into my back pocket, and away I went.

I can see in retrospect that it was when I took my eyes off Christ.

Did you put on the back burner all the things you had picked up from *The Great Controversy* and those other books?

I thought at the time that I still had a righteous heart. I thought I had a connection with Christ. But I didn't. I was just maybe looking for excuses, and I found them. I was looking at all the negative things. It was basically that I was following other people rather than my own conscience and the Word.

Did you go back to your old lifestyle?

Gradually I just stopped coming to church almost altogether. When Cindy had people over, I would leave. And then I went completely back into the world as far as occasionally smoking pot and drinking and smoking, not giving a hoot about anything or anybody. I was completely avoiding any contact with anyone in the church.

At that point, Cindy's and my relationship, although on the surface it looked OK, was pretty much in a shambles. I resented her, I resented the church, and I even resented myself. It was just a real hard time in my life.

Did you have any contact with the offshoot groups Cindy was involved with?

That's basically what led me out the door, at least the one offshoot group. I did a lot of work for them with my bulldozer, and I had my log skidder up there a few times. It was basically that crowd that led me out the door. I mean, some of the things you wouldn't believe, the way they would talk about the pastors.

Right now, if I go to a church and the pastor has an off-the-wall sermon or an intellectual sermon that I can't grasp 100 percent, I can still get something out of it. We can't be so closed that we can't get something out of the spoken word. But back then it got to the point where people would come over and we'd sit there and nitpick the sermon or the way he acted or the way he combed his hair. The devil was after me, but those people helped a lot in my slide out of the church.

How long did you stay away?

Probably four or five years. During that time, Cindy and I were separated for about a year. And I had slid so far down in the dark tunnel, it's a miracle, by the grace of God, that we're back together. It was too long a time.

What was that year like?

It was very dark and very lonely. I cried a lot. Got in a few fistfights. I'd completely reverted back to the times before I'd been converted. I didn't care about anybody or anything. It was the grace of God and Cindy's prayers and my family's prayers that brought me back.

What finally brought us back together was that I figured, hey, I'd better get my act together and get back to at least living in the same town, or we'll never get back together. So I moved my meager possessions back to the town where Cindy was. We occasionally started seeing each other because of the kids, and one thing led to another. I started going back to church, and here we are. I have to thank God.

Both of you seemed to have a different attitude at that point of reconciliation. Is that true?

Definitely. I remember the first time I saw Cindy after being apart for about a year. She was at her grandmother's house, and she had on these pretty pink slacks and attractive sweater. It was like, hey, there's my sweetheart!

We had gotten so much into the negatives. Cindy didn't get as much into the negativism as I did against the church. She was a little off-base, but I was the one who really went away. I think the devil has a way of getting at the head of the house in particular. Cindy grew up that year, but I grew up ten times as much in some ways. But there was a marked difference even in her countenance. You could see the change.

How did you go back into the church?

I pretty much just started going back. There were a few tense times. One of the pastors wanted to sit us down and give us some counseling and stuff. That was right after I went back. It was all right, but it was not what was needed. What I needed was someone to shake my hand and say, "Hey, I'm glad to see you." I needed to be befriended and loved and nur-

tured. After surgery you need some recovery time and
some therapy. I think therapy of the soul—friendship—means an awful lot, just knowing that someone cares about you and prays about you.

**Was that pastor trying to do this the day you
got back?**
Pretty much. I don't know if we were tagged or la-
beled or what. I know quite a few in the small conservative church where the split happened were saying, "Watch these people, they're renegades."

**How long did it take for you to think of your-
self as a full member again?**
Probably less than a year. There were still people
who were trying to grab us into one camp or another.
But something in my heart told me that the Lord had
forgiven me and that I felt all right with Him.

Have you run into many problems since then?
Yeah, there's been a few here in our church. There
are always people. But the one thing I can say is that I
have to keep my eyes on Christ. There are always going
to be people who are into some of these other groups.
They want you to read something or take you aside.
But if we can keep our eyes on Christ, we'll do all right.
We have some friends in the church in the next
town—I talked to one on the phone tonight. He kind
of chose sides when the church split, and I gave him
some advice to let it go. Don't carry that baggage with
you, because it will harm you. Keep studying, and
don't be taken in by it.

Do you have any regrets?
I think it's been like getting a disease. You may be

cured of it, but you're going to have scars, maybe some deformity. But we are wiser and healthier now that we are older. I think if we had not started going to some of those meetings, at least for me anyway, that cast doubt on the church as a body, even though things aren't perfect in the church—if we had stayed with the printed word and the books and kept a balance, I don't think any of this would have happened. Who knows? With my psyche and mentality, I might have been converting people instead of dragging them away from the church. But it was the steps of guilt by association, I think.

Do you have gifts that you give to the church now?

I think just mainly looking people in the eye and giving them an honest smile and shaking their hand. Cindy's much more of a witnesser than I am, but I like to encourage people, compliment them, just sit down and talk with them. I'm still pretty much laid back.

One of the biggest things that's happened to me was going on *Insight*/Maranatha's mission trip with my son last summer. It taught me a whole lot of patience and a whole lot of understanding of teenagers. I look at the youth of our church now with a whole different attitude and outlook. I don't look at their long hair or their unkempt appearance or what they're wearing. I look them in the eye. I was saying to a guy last weekend, even if I'd had to spend five thousand bucks, it would have been worth it for my growth. Like going to college for ten years, those two weeks.

Are you going on another trip?

I'm going to try to get my wife to go. I wanted to take my kids anyway. We'll see what happens. It was a challenge for me emotionally. I cried three times, and they weren't tears of joy. It was a growth experience. I mean, I got stretched!

What have you said to people you've met who don't know much about the problems you've come through?

Well, I've said, "Buyer beware." The group I got involved with was taking Sister White's sentences out of context. If you read the whole chapter of what they're quoting from, you can get the big picture. But I've been honest with people and said that this selective quoting is a bunch of garbage. They might sound good, they might look good, and some of what they have to say might make sense. But the whole package is not worth the paper it's printed on. They were trying to lead people out of the church, taking their tithe, and when we needed help, they were not there to help us.

Are new converts vulnerable to that? They might think someone like you is the problem.

Well, new converts are generally, whether they've come into the church with no Christian background or come in from another church, on fire. They think, *Hey, this is some new material here.* It's like a Broadway producer getting a jewel of a script. He's excited, he wants to hire a cast and put a production on. It's the same with new converts. They know some things, they want to know more, and they're ripe for the plucking.

I've seen it time and again—an on-fire couple who aren't firmly grounded, and these offshoot guys will grab onto them and start yanking their chain.

Can we help new members be discerning?

I remember when Cindy and I came in, and that elderly lady gave us those books. Had she sat us down and said, "Keep your eyes on Jesus," if someone had made me aware, if someone had said, "There's some groups out there who have a little truth but they're going to try to lead you astray." I don't know how you could actually come out and say that without offending somebody. But there's got to be a way. Maybe to take new people in the church and befriend them honestly and with an open heart and guide them along. And if they see anyone trying to lead them away, let them know in a kind, gentle way, "Just keep your eyes on Christ."

And the older members having a relationship with the newcomers would be important?

Most definitely. They should take them under their wing and study with them. And keep their names off the mailing list!

When we first came in, it started with one little group who published a little tiny newsletter. I think our name went from that mailing list onto a couple more, and pretty soon you've got all this junk coming in. And we're reading it and going to these other meetings and stuff. I can just see the steps, *boom, boom, boom.*

How do you look at the future?

Our main concern is our teenage children, making sure they're happy in the Lord and in church. Just trying to be a conservative mediating factor in the great controversy. Knowing where we've been, I think we're pretty wise in Adventism and Christianity, probably pretty conservative still, me even more so after going through some of the things we did.

I can see eventually a time like Sister White warned about. There's going to be a shaking, and it's going to

be ugly. If you're not firmly founded in Christ, it's
going to be a real hard time for you.

Questions

1. How can mature Christians help recent converts
to prepare for differences they will encounter in the
Seventh-day Adventist Church?

2. What is the best approach to handling a serious
rift in a church congregation?

3. What advice is appropriate to give members who
sympathize with the complaints of offshoot groups?

4. Is your congregation preparing for a shaking?
What specific plans does it have? Are the plans being
used?

5. What should be the response of the church to
offshoot groups?

Chapter 9

John

---

early thirties, single, teacher, musician

Did you grow up in the Seventh-day Adventist Church?

Yes, I did. I can remember going to church way, way back when I was in first and second grade. That foundation my parents instilled in me at that early age, I believe, was beneficial to me later on in life.

Do you think you really understood what you were doing when you joined the church?

I think so. I was nine years old when I was baptized the first time. As a matter of fact, I just reflected on this yesterday at a concert I gave. I carry my baptismal certificate in my Bible and use it as a witness to the young people I meet. I had the Sabbath School program yesterday for the juniors and earliteens and gave them a brief background of my life, but I didn't go in too deep with them. I showed them the baptismal certificate because I am really proud of it.

At nine years of age, I truly believed I was well on my way to being an Adventist my entire life. We had all the early teachings that little kids are taught. I knew Seventh-day Adventism at that age. I knew that Adventism was right because my folks had led me to know that.

So you believe that you really knew God at that age?

I really did. I truly believe that. As a little kid I was singing with my brother and two sisters a lot— I'm the youngest. We used to sing together a lot. When Friday evening came, we'd always have family worship, and music was an important part of that. The four of us would even have a little program we did for Mom and Dad on Sabbath afternoons.

Sabbath was a celebration day for us. We would go to church and come home for lunch. Then Mom and Dad would rest for a while. While they were napping, we would plan for the Sabbath afternoon programs. When Mom and Dad would wake up, we'd have our own prayer, and we'd have our own little church service, kind of our own children's church. We did all sorts of things in the living room. We would perform these afternoon "church" services for Mom and Dad—always with lots of singing and Bible stories we would tell.

Did you go to Adventist schools?

We really didn't have the opportunity to go to church school at that time. I guess it was available to us, but it was something we as kids discussed with our folks—if that's really what we wanted to do and if that was the best route for us.

Attending public schools gave us the opportunity to become involved in sports. And sports was the love of my life. I wanted to be a part of the soccer team; I wanted to be a part of the basketball team—and all the other teams. These were the first challenges where I had to deal with Sabbath.

I can well remember when I was in my freshman year in high school. The soccer coach really wanted me to come out for the team, but I told him I couldn't practice on Saturdays. I told him it was my Sabbath day, and he said, "Well, you can still come and try out for the team. If you make the team, then we'll go from there."

Well, I made the team, and he really wanted me as a starter. I told him, "Coach, I am not going to be able to practice on Saturdays." And he allowed that. I wasn't too popular with the other players on the team, because they had to be there on Saturdays. So that was the first obstacle I ran into in high school.

I want you to know that I believe kids can be a witness in public school.

During that time, I was also heavily involved with music. I was still singing with my brother and sisters, and we were doing a lot of singing in our church. And, of course, we were still attending church regularly. Then in my junior year in high school, I was nominated to be a part of the all-state chorus. I was really excited about that. I made the all-state chorus as a baritone. I was able to be a part of that during my senior year—you do the audition in your junior year, and in your senior year you get to attend.

In my senior year I went to all-state chorus at a convention center in the state capital. While there, I auditioned for all-eastern chorus as well, which covered the entire East Coast of the United States. I made it to the finals—number 16. But they only chose eight. So I made it up to the final cut, and then I was beat out, which was fine with me.

Another exciting thing that happened as a result was that the music director was from the University of Miami, and he offered me a full scholarship—a music scholarship—at his school. But I would have had to major in music. I didn't want music to be my entire life at that time, because I knew sports was a major part of my life as well. And since I enjoyed singing on the side, that's the route I took. I decided to stick to sports and also enjoy music. And that's basically where I ended up after my senior year in high school.

What initially led you away from the church?

When I graduated from high school, I was working for McDonald's. I worked my way up and became the manager, and I thought this was the time for me to sort of spread my wings a little bit. I really didn't want to go to college immediately, because I wasn't sure what field I wanted to pursue. So for about five years I was sort of feeling my way around.

I was deeply involved in tennis. I played every weekend, and finally I had to make a decision. I had to ask myself, "Do I really want to play tennis on the Sabbath? Do I want to go to church?" I decided I would play both parts. I told myself, "I'll keep going to church, but I'll make sure that my tennis matches are scheduled in the afternoon. Then I can still attend church in the morning."

People saw me at church on Sabbath. I was there physically. But that was my way of getting around the fact that people wouldn't understand about me playing on the Sabbath. I continued doing that for some time. For five years my entire time was consumed by tennis and tennis friends, people around me who basically influenced me to believe there was a better way of life out there than having to go to church. At that time it didn't matter to me if I went to church on Saturday or Sunday. It just didn't matter what kind of religion I had. Just so I believed in God.

Well, when I turned twenty-three, I left home and attended the state university on a tennis scholarship. From that point on, my folks didn't know whether I was still attending church or not. And the church definitely took a back seat in my life.

How long were you out of the church?

During that time period of eighteen to twenty-three years of age, my folks were constantly hounding me that I shouldn't be playing tennis on Saturdays, that I should be in church instead. And I said to them, "You know, this [tennis] is something that could really be big, and right now this has a priority in my life." So they allowed me to make my own decisions.

I had reached an age when I thought I could make my own decisions. So I made my decision, but I was out of the church. Oh, I was still attending church off and on. As a matter of fact, I rarely showed up in the church for about three years. I went sporadically, but I was just playing a game.

What sort of life did you have away from the church?

I still remember the times when I was out of the church. My sister, Mom or Dad, or somebody would say, "They'd like us to sing for church next week. Can you be there?"

On such occasions when I had a tennis tournament, I would tell the tennis people, "Look, I can't play at this particular tournament until 2 or 3 o'clock in the afternoon. So you need to schedule me later in the day since I have an obligation that morning." Then I would go and sing that morning and play in the tournament in the afternoon.

I loved singing. Although I knew I really wasn't the strong Christian I should have been, it didn't even bother me to get up in front of the church and sing.

Music was that important to you?

Oh yes. I tried to spread my music wings a little bit more because I really enjoyed music a lot. Many people suggested that I ought to audition for some of the Broadway shows that were being put on by community drama groups in the local theaters. At that time I was still working on my bachelor's degree and had certain requirements that I had to fulfill in liberal arts, so I took a theater class. We had to have 100 hours of theater work to earn the highest grade. If you have an audition for a show and you make it, you get to add up all the rehearsal time and the hours on stage, and you can get those hours pretty quick.

Well, I auditioned for one of those shows and landed a lead musical part. I soon had my 100 hours. Of course, the show was on Thursday, Friday, and Saturday nights, with a Sunday matinee. So it meant being at the theater on Friday and Saturday evenings. But still I did it. It was great fun for me. I continued auditioning, and soon I was doing theater productions, singing at weddings, and still singing in the church as well.

Tell me about any significant contacts you had with church members while you were away from the church.

I really didn't have any significant contacts with the church. At least, not when I graduated from college. I can remember the time I became close to the pastor of our church. We became friends. He wanted to know more about my life because he had been hearing numerous rumors about me. If there was anyone in the church with whom I had a significant contact, it would be that man. He persistently preached to me and made some sense to me.

He was a middle-aged guy, I guess about ten years older than I am. He was like a mentor. He was someone I could look up to, someone who was a role model for me. And once I got to know him, he was not just my pastor but my friend, and he still continues to be my friend today.

Well, he had been hearing a lot of rumors about me and the things I had been doing on Sabbath. Finally, one day he called and said he wanted to meet with me. And I thought, *Oh boy, I know what this is about.*

He came to the house, and I'll never forget the visit. We had set up a time, and I was a bit nervous. We weren't real close at this time, but I could feel there was a kind of camaraderie between the two of us. When he came, we went downstairs in the family room because I didn't want my folks to hear what we were discussing. This particular interview with him was private!

He asked me what I was doing, and I didn't lie to him. I was very open and honest with him. This was the first real test I had put myself to with someone. Finally I opened up and shared my inner thoughts, which I had kept hidden for all these years, with someone I could trust. He was the first person to whom I communicated openly about everything.

What did you think about the church in general while you were separated from it?

When I was living near the university, I still attended church occasionally because I felt that the Holy Spirit never left me, even though I did some crazy and stupid things. I can remember waking up on Sabbath mornings and going to the local church for Sabbath morning service. No, I didn't do that all the time. I would go maybe once every two months.

Church was still part of life for me. Often I would hear that small voice saying, "Why don't you get up and go to church today?" and so I would do that. Of course, when I went home for weekends and holidays, I always attended church with my folks. I didn't want them to think that I wasn't going to church. But when I was away, I did my own thing, and I went to church only when I felt like it.

When did you first think of returning to the church on a more regular basis? What prompted it?

I can clearly remember the night. It was Friday evening. I had been living near the university during the summers for about three or four years, coaching tennis at a club there. I remember going into this bar, which I frequented almost every night with my friends, to watch *Jeopardy* and *Wheel of Fortune*. They had a deal there. If you could answer the final jeopardy question, you got a free drink. So I'd always go in and play *Jeopardy*, hoping to win a free drink.

I remember looking at my watch. My watch had the days of the week on it, and when I happened to look down, it was just starting to switch days. You could see the hour hand on the watch gradually switching over to Saturday, and I knew it was Sabbath. I started thinking, "Wonder what Mom and Dad are doing at home right now?"

I knew what they were doing—the same thing my other family members were doing. I knew they were all enjoying the Sabbath day, and here I was sitting in a bar. Well, at that moment it really hit me.

You know, they say that the Holy Spirit leaves you when you go into those places. I truly believe that was *not* the case with me, because when I went in there something—Someone—made me look at my watch. There were too many things inside me saying, "Why don't you go home? Why don't you just go home?"

So I did just that, that very instant. I said to myself, "It's time for a change. You've got to search your life; you've been through an awful lot. It's time to get back on track."

So I went back to my apartment, packed up all my belongings, and went home that night. And since then I have been living at home with my folks.

I started attending church regularly. My pastor friend made several visits to my parents' house, and I laid everything on the line with him. He came to know about my drinking, all the intimate details of drugs, and some of the other things I had been involved with.

What was it like when you were returning to church? Did you run into any problems?

I don't think you really want to know this, but I will give an honest opinion.

I was not very well liked at church. My pastor and his wife were fantastic people. They were the people I really clung to, because the reception I got from a lot of people was ridicule. Like they were saying, "What's he doing back here?"

That's what I sensed. Whether that's what they felt or not, that's what I sensed. I didn't feel a lot of love. Even to this day I don't feel a lot of love. But I know where my heart is with the Lord, and that's the thing I was really having a struggle with at the beginning.

But the pastor and his wife made sure to contact me every day, and we became close friends. They knew this story was going to be a success story and not a backsliding story. Later on, after my rebaptism, they kind of built walls around me so I wouldn't go back to my old ways again. Satan was trying harder once I accepted the Lord back into my life. The experiences they gave me stuck with me and have given me a lot of focus in life.

I have done a lot of maturing and a lot of growing up in the church. But unfortunately, still there are people who know my background and they still have that—I don't want to say it—but they have that real bad taste in their mouths because they know what I was and they don't want to accept what I am now. But that's OK.

Was everyone like that?

No. I can't say that about all, because there were some people who welcomed me with open arms. I accept those who didn't and still don't, but I would like people to put my past in the background. I really believe the Lord has opened a lot of doors and has given me many people, not only in our church but within other churches, to whom I have been able to cling for friendship and understanding. If they know my background, and a lot of them do, they have forgiven me, and I truly appreciate them.

What happened to your interest in sports and music?

After the reconversion, I wanted to be rebaptized. I wanted to start the new year out right because I thought it was a new beginning for me. So on January 2, the first Sabbath of the new year in 1993, I was rebaptized.

Some time before that, I had read an article about entering a talent search that was sponsored by the Heritage Singers. My folks bugged me and bugged me to enter this search thing. But I told them, "You know there are so many talented musicians at the Adventist colleges, many music majors, and I'm just an amateur."

But they kept talking to me. The constant bugging came not only from my folks but also from my pastor and his wife. They kept saying, "Do it, John. You never know."

Finally I decided that even though there are many music majors and I am an amateur, this is an amateur talent search, and I should go for it.

So I entered this talent search, and to make a long story short, in May when they announced the winner, I received a phone call here at home on a Friday evening. And it was so ironic that all the people who were involved in my reconversion were at the house that night. It was just like the Lord wanted it that way.

When the phone rang, I picked it up. It was Max Mace on the other end of the line and he said, "John, we want to tell you that you are the first-prize winner in the vocal division of our Christian talent search for the solo division."

I said, "What! Are you sure you've got the right number?"

Then he said, "Yes, you are John, aren't you?"

And I said, "Yes," but I couldn't believe it was happening to me.

The next Monday I got a phone call at work about 1:30 in the afternoon, and it was Max Mace again. When I heard his voice, I said, "See, you did have the wrong person, didn't you?"

And he said, "No, John, I called you back to let you know that you are our grand-prize winner! Out of the three divisions in the talent search, we had to pick a top winner. You are the grand-prize winner."

That prize entitled me to record a compact disc.

You can't tell me I am not a true believing Christian, that I don't believe in God. Things happen in our lives I truly believe are for a reason. And people, too—people come into our lives for a reason. God places them there for us. I've learned that God wants it that way. I believe that He allowed this to happen in my life, because for me, entering that talent search was a shot in the dark.

I know God allowed this to happen in my life, because my experience with music just mushroomed from there. About a year later, the producer of *It Is Written* happened to pick up my CD on the West Coast. He asked me to come out for an audition, to do a taping with *It Is Written*, and to appear on the program. Well, I made it through the audition, and I appeared on *It Is Written*. For the last few years I have been singing with them. I performed on Net '96 and recently received a letter asking me to work with the Voice of Prophecy on some of their programs. I have accepted and will be appearing with them seven times next year as a vocalist.

So my music experience has really taken off. I've done no seeking of this at all. The Lord has just opened a lot of doors for me. I am so thankful He is part of my life now. It's amazing that so many doors have been opened. You just can't imagine. I laugh and I think, *Wow, how the pieces of the puzzle have fit into place!*

Where do you think you will be five years from now? What do you think you will be doing?

You know, I really don't know what I will be doing. And it doesn't really matter to me.

I've learned a lot through my reconversion and from many people I've been around. Mark Finley has been a great influence on my life. He takes things a day at a time and doesn't like to predict the future. Right now I'm very content with my life, even though sometimes the future looks a little scary. I'm content to live one day at a time.

Where the future takes me in five years from now, I don't know. I don't worry about it. I'm leaving that in the Lord's hands. Wherever He leads me, I am willing to go. At times I'm a little afraid to say that, because I know there are things He's brought into my life I always said I never wanted to do. And just when I doubt, it seems like a particular door starts to open.

Am I a little scared of what He may have in store for me? Yes. Maybe. On numerous occasions I've made the statement that I would never go full time in music, though at times I wince when I say it, because there are so many opportunities that are becoming available. And it has nothing to do with me making phone calls. The phone calls keep coming to me. So I've left everything in His hands. Wherever He leads me from here, that's where I'm willing to go.

What would you like to say to people who have left the church and have no plans to return?

"If they have no plans to return"—that's a wrong statement to make. I said the same words. If they have no intention whatsoever to come back to the church—that's going to come back and haunt them. I can guarantee you that. If they truly have the foundation, the Lord and the Holy Spirit won't leave them alone—that's what brought me back. That still, small voice saying, "What are you doing?" will bring them back.

I don't know what my advice would be to them. Maybe that the decisions I made were human decisions and I know they were wrong, but when I finally allowed the Lord to come back into my life and start making the decisions for me, to help me make the right decisions, things were different. He gives us the choice; we make the decisions. When I finally started to seek Him, His influence on those decisions took over and controlled my life. Before, my faith in Him was very, very small—and I knew that.

I think I would say, "Get close to the Lord; give Him a chance. Because He gave me a chance to come back. There's a time when the Holy Spirit will depart from our lives. Don't let it get to that point. You've got to continue hanging in there even though it may look rough. That's what brought me back."

What would you say to lifelong church members, to people who have never left the church?

I know there are some people who have never left the church. It amazes me they've stuck it out and were so faithful to God and God was so good to them that they never turned their backs on Him. They never let Satan throw those little darts at them. I admire those people. I respect those people so much.

And I respect those people who can see a sinner leave the church and come back and welcome him with open arms. Those are the people whom I truly want to thank. Those who have been by my side and those who gave me the strength to move on. What I want to say to them more than anything else is Thanks.

What about those who don't receive sinners with open arms?

I've really learned to block that out. Do I dislike them? No. Because I believe that that is something they are struggling with. That is what they have to come to grips with.

It says in Matthew 7, "Judge not lest ye be judged." I truly believe that some of those people are having a real hard time judging my life instead of looking into their own hearts. Do I avoid them? No. If anything, I want to be around them more because I want them to see there is a change in my life. There is Somebody in my life now whom they need to meet. I'm not trying to say that in a vindictive way, but if they are truly loving people, they will know that my Lord is a very compassionate Man and a very loving God.

If we want to be truly Christlike, we need to put those awful feelings away that we sometimes have in our hearts about other people. We need to say, "I am looking at the person he is now, not what he was before."

This used to be very frustrating, but the Lord has given me peace of mind. I can now walk into the church regardless of what may be said and done. I can hold my head high because I know where I stand with the Lord, and at the judgment day I know where I will be.

What's your advice to new converts?

When I was rebaptized, I basically felt as though I was a new member. When reconversion takes place, you're excited, you're on fire for the Lord. You just want to take on everything. And I still remember that was the case with me for about six or seven months until Satan really started to try me again. No doubt Satan will not give up on you, because he knows when we start to slip, and he will find a way to sneak back into our lives.

The thing I would recommend to them the most is to continue to pray daily. Prayer is a big thing, at least in my life. I pray constantly that the Lord will give me focus. Give me some type of direction. Give me the signs and trust me. He's done that. The more faith I have in Him, the more He's been able to do in my life.

Sometimes when we as new converts look back at what we used to be, Satan will bring doubts into our hearts. He will start bringing people into our lives who'd say, "Hey, its OK to still do that." The one thing you need to realize is that you should not put yourself in situations where you are going to be tempted to do those things that you were doing before.

John, what are you doing for the Lord?

Right now? My music keeps me very busy, but you know I'd say that is fine. When I go to these places to give concerts, sometimes I am so tired and exhausted that I just bow my head and say, "Lord, give me strength, because You know how I'm feeling. I am weary right now, You need to pick me up."

And every time I do that it's amazing how the second wind comes along. I just look up and say Thank You, Lord. This is an experience whereby I am able to witness for the Lord and meet some of the most wonderful people I have ever met in my life.

You might say that music took you out of the church, and now it has brought you back. But what if music left your life, if you couldn't sing or give concerts, what would you do?

It's true, music has indeed opened many doors. To answer part of the question, God has given each one of us some talent, and I know music is a God-given talent to me. I've never taken formal training nor am I professional like some of the Adventist musicians I've become acquainted with.

I think the reason the Lord is doing this to me is that He apparently sees some type of talent He wants to bring out. And I don't believe the Lord would take music away from me even if I am not faithful. I think He would continue to open doors. But if the music should end, I think the Lord will find another way to use me in the church as long as I would allow Him to do so.

I've had many ups and downs. More downs than ups, but the ups are starting to catch up. If we turn our lives over to Jesus, He will take *that* life, whatever its condition, and will mold it to be what He wants it to be. If we allow Him to take full control of our lives, we just can't imagine where He will take us.

Questions

1. How can the church encourage young people who do not attend Adventist schools to develop their talents and gifts, particularly during their high school years? In what ways did John's church help him, if any?

2. John received a tennis scholarship to attend a state university. How can the church encourage young adults who have such abilities? Should Adventist colleges offer sports scholarships? Explain your answer.

3. Generally speaking, the church discourages competition, but John found great satisfaction in competing in sports and music. How can the church encourage young adults to use their talents without emphasizing competition?

4. John describes feelings of being rejected by many members of his church. Do we sometimes reject or at the least ignore those who return? Why? Describe some ways church members might demonstrate love and support for people like John who have determined to turn their lives around and use their talents for God.

5. What role does the church have in drug education for juniors and earliteens? Should the church encourage those who have used drugs to tell their stories to kids? Explain your answer.

------ Chapter 10 ------

Ray

---
midfifties, married, farmer

Were you raised as an Adventist?

Yes. My father wasn't. I never remember him going to church. But my mother was a good Christian woman. She took us to church as youngsters, and we enjoyed Sabbath School very much. We lived five miles away from the church, and since we didn't always have a ride or if Mom couldn't go, my two brothers and I would walk to church on Sabbath and walk back home. We really enjoyed Sabbath School!

Did you go to Adventist schools?

We attended church school just for one year, but it wasn't a real good experience. I really don't have much to say about that. We attended the public school near our home.

My mother tried to bring us up in the right way. She taught us to keep the Sabbath. We worked during the summers, paid our tithes, and enjoyed our

Sabbath School classes. We had good Sabbath School teachers, and I can remember doing things we really looked forward to.

How old were you when you were baptized? Do you think you were a converted Christian?

We were baptized as children. I was probably around thirteen or fourteen years old. And as I look back on it, I probably wasn't ready to be baptized. At least not the way I feel now about how we should have been when we were baptized.

What was it that took you away from the church?

I graduated from high school and began to work on Sabbaths. I felt as though I had to work on the Sabbath. It seems like once you work on one Sabbath, it's easy to work on another and another. And then I wasn't going to church at all.

I was doing orchard work. I worked in the same orchard for many years, about thirty years altogether. I started picking strawberries at this place when I was eight or nine years old. And I worked there every summer. My brothers and I also worked there in the evenings after school. We bought our own school clothes and paid for our lunches. We paid our own way by working evenings and in the summertime.

When I graduated, I began to work full time at this orchard and did a lot of truck driving. I would work in the orchard during the day and drive a truck at nights delivering produce. So there were weeks when I would work about eighty to one hundred hours a week.

I enjoyed the work. But there was never a time when I didn't think of wanting to go back to the church. I knew that if the Lord came, I would be lost. Occasionally I would see one of the church members, because we sold produce from the orchard and farm, and we often had people from the church who would come to buy apples, sweet corn, and other things. Sometimes when I would see some of the church leaders, I felt like hiding from them. These individuals were very good Christians, and they always stood out in my mind as good people. But I was doing wrong, and I knew it.

I was out of the church for twenty-five years.

What kept you away from church? Working on Sabbaths?

Well, not only that. After I graduated, I also began associating with different friends, and I began to drink and ride motorcycles and did other things with them that caused me to drift away from the church. At eighteen or nineteen I got married. We soon had a daughter, then a son. So at a very young age I had a family to support and had to work. With all that responsibility, I took on an evening job and worked every evening for five or six hours for an extra twenty dollars. Just some extra money to keep the family going. But I bought a lot of things I didn't need, like a motorcycle.

And I was away from home too much. Instead of working long days or running around with my friends, I should have spent more time with my family in the evenings. I realize as I grow older that there are a lot of things I should have done that I didn't do to be a better father and husband. We were married seven years then divorced. Without God at the center of our lives, it just will not work.

Did any of the people from church talk to you about coming back?

Sometimes I felt as if I wanted to hide from them,

and I think the reason is I was afraid they were going to ask me about coming back to church. But I can't remember them ever saying anything about it. They might have said a time or two that they missed me or something like that. They didn't say, "You're going to be lost if you don't get back to church" or anything like that. I didn't feel condemned by church members.

Did you ever think about the church at all during those twenty-five years?

Yes, I'd think about the church many a time and believed I was going to be lost if probation closed. But I continued to live the way I was living. Sometimes you feel the Lord's not going to come now and you've got a few more years. So you just want to have fun, at least what I thought was fun, for a few more years.

I married again and moved to this farm where my wife was living with her father. Some time later, we had a daughter. But I really didn't change the way I was living. I began to drink a lot and rode off on my motorcycle with my friends. I spent less and less time with my wife and family, and finally it came to a point where my wife and I separated a couple of times.

I can clearly remember the last drink I had. It was a Saturday, and it seemed as if I had gone to the very bottom. My wife and I were getting on each other's nerves. By this time I had moved out and gone to an apartment. And I remember that night, climbing out of the bed and getting down on my knees and praying, "Lord, if you take me back home, and if my wife and I can work things out, I will never touch another drink, and I'll get back to church." And I can honestly say, I never had another drink after that.

What happened when you went back home?

We talked a long time, and she agreed to try again. And from that day on we've been together with very few problems.

How did you get back to church?

When I was out of the church, many times my mom would say, "Ray, wouldn't you like the pastor to come and have Bible studies with you?"

And I would say, "No, I'm not ready for any Bible studies."

But after my wife and I got back together, I felt like having Bible studies. So the pastor came to our home. Then we had a Revelation seminar at the church right after that, and I attended all those meetings. And at that time I felt I wanted to be rebaptized.

How did your wife take all this? Was she an Adventist?

No, but my wife had already started to attend the Adventist Church with my mom, probably back in the 70s. She had been attending church without me for quite a few years.

Was it OK with you for her to go to church?

Oh yes, it was all right with me for her to go to church. I was glad she did. But I never gave it a whole lot of thought at that time or ever wanted to go with her. Because at that time I thought I was happy with what I was doing, with the way I was living.

Did she encourage you to come with her to church on Sabbath mornings?

No, not much. No, she was just happy to go to church and went practically every Saturday. She was happy to go with my mom. She didn't hassle me about church at all.

After you got back together with your wife, did you keep your promise? Did you go back to church right away?

Yes. Even while my wife and I were taking Bible studies together, I began to attend church right away. And from that day until this very day, I can remember missing only one day of church, and that was because I was sick. On some occasions we may have been away, but wherever we were, we went to church.

How did the church members respond when you went back to church?

I can remember a couple of church members who talked to me. I especially remember one brother saying to me, "Brother, I have been praying for you for many a year." Hearing this, I felt cold chills go all the way to my toes. He also said, "Now which of your other brothers do you want us to pray for?"

And I can still remember another brother telling me. I love that brother so much. He said, "I want to tell you something, Ray. As you come back to church, don't you look at nobody, no man or no woman in the church. You keep your eyes on Jesus." And I know that was real good advice.

Did you run into any problems when you came back to the church? Did you have any problems keeping Sabbath?

Yes, indeed, we had a lot of problems. After I came back to the church, I became the manager at the orchard and tried to work things out so I wouldn't have to be there on Saturdays. Everything seemed to be going real well, and we didn't have any Sabbath problems. But about two years later the owner died, and his son and grandson bought out the daughters and the owner's wife. One Sunday right after that they called me in and said there were going to be some changes; that I would be required to work on Sabbaths. They gave me until the next morning to make up my mind about what I would do.

Well, I prayed a lot that night. The next day I went to see them. My mind was made up. If they wanted me to work on Sabbaths, that was going to be my last day there. I had already talked to my wife about it. And so when I went back on Monday morning, I told them I could not work on Saturday so I was quitting.

So here you are. You have a wife, you have children, a family to take care of, and no job. What did you do?

It gives you an awful funny feeling after working so many years for one company just to quit in one day's time. I didn't really know exactly what I was going to do.

We'd thought of doing other things, like going into the orchard business ourselves. Before he died, my father-in-law had told us that if we wanted to go out and plant trees and get an orchard started on his farm, he would give us some land he owned in the next state.

We started that but just didn't feel that the Lord was blessing in going that particular direction. We also planted strawberries and later some sweet corn. It's a long story, how it all worked out, but the next year my wife's father died, and the farm had to be sold. The Lord provided for us, and we worked out a deal whereby we could purchase the farm and run it ourselves. We were able to purchase 168 acres of land

and the house and buildings at that time. And we are still growing vegetables here today. The Lord has blessed us every year since then.

As a young man you were drawn away from the church by your work and by relationships with people who were not Adventists. What is your life like now, especially in the summertime?

We really are very busy during the summer. Starting in June, but mainly July, August, and September are our busiest months. Like I said, I love this kind of work. My wife works hard too. My youngest daughter and son-in-law—they have their own home here on the place—they also help us on the farm.

Working here on your own farm is almost just like owning your home and planting a garden and just enjoying the work. I enjoy this work very much, but at times I feel I am spending too much time working. It's so hard to get up early in the morning when I work so late at nights that I find it hard to make time to read and pray. I truly believe that sometimes we are trying to do too many things at one time. I am praying hard that the Lord will help me so I will make more time to get involved in giving Bible studies.

I know you had some experiences with floods here last spring. Tell me a little bit about that.

This has probably been the worst year ever for us. I've lived on this farm for twenty-eight years. Somewhere around there. And last year was the worst year I've ever seen.

My father-in-law came here in 1936 and lived through the big flood that year. They tell me it was about as bad as the two floods we had here last year.

The year's troubles started out early. To begin with,

there was a major flood in January that covered up most of the strawberries. We spent days getting all the mud off them, re-strawing them, and working on them day after day. Then we had a freeze in May that killed the biggest part of the strawberry patch. After that we had real wet weather all summer, but in spite of that, we had a very good corn crop, probably the best we've ever had. Also the cantaloupes and tomatoes were fairly good.

After all this, we had another bad flood in September that pretty much took all the cantaloupes and tomatoes we had left and ruined our pumpkins. We normally harvest 150 to 160 tons of pumpkins, but this year we barely harvested 20 tons.

Through it all the Lord has still blessed us, and I think we still had a very good year.

Anyhow, everything belongs to Him. If He wants the floods to come, it will flood. There is nothing we can do about it. We just have to have faith in Him. And that's where I am today, believing He will take care of us.

That's quite a story. Now, you said your wife came back to church with you. What about your children? What happened to them?

I can remember my two daughters attending church at that time. They still do. I don't remember how old my one daughter was, but she had her own daughter by that time. And I can still remember my granddaughter, she was maybe around four years old then, I can remember being baptized that day and walking down the aisle and hearing her saying, "Angels are singing in heaven today, Pap." It was so beautiful.

How involved are you in your church today?

I am an elder in the church, and just this past year

I took a course with our new pastor on giving Bible studies. Right now our church is trying to get involved in prison ministries. We are hoping we can get something going soon. It seems like it's so hard.

I do know we are living in the last days. I feel that we as Seventh-day Adventists are the Israel of today, and we are to do just as Israel was to do back when God brought them out of Egypt. And I feel we are failing at this point and not reaching out as we should.

Would you say you've learned anything of value as a result of your twenty-five years away from the church?

Yes, I've learned one thing for sure, that it's something we don't want to put off. I am just so thankful God didn't come during those twenty-five years I was away from the church, or I would have been lost. I think about it a lot and about many out there who are not going to have another twenty-five years to come back. We need to do all we can to help others to know that soon the Lord is coming, and it's today that we need to come back and allow the Lord to come into our hearts. We need to make the changes that need to be made in our lives and not put it off.

You probably run into former Adventists now and then, people who may have grown up in the church when you did but are not in the church now and probably aren't even thinking about coming back to church. What would you say to those folk?

I think I'd be careful not to do anything to discourage them like when I was away. I think of the Adventists I came in contact with at that time. I pray every day that the Lord will send His Holy Spirit and give me words to speak at the right time. And I pray that when the opportunity should come, and it has come many times, that the Lord will give me words to speak. I can't remember exactly what it was I said, but I know I have come in contact with a number of former Adventists, and I've said things to them I feel came from the Lord.

What about the lifelong members in the church today? Do you have any words for those who have never left the church?

I look at the church a lot of times and ask myself where have we gone, considering the years I had been away. Where have we gone during all these years? I haven't seen the growth I think we ought to have in our church. I feel that so many times we just come to church Sabbath after Sabbath and we hear a good sermon and do nothing about it. Many times we've had good pastors, and we've had beautiful sermons; yet I feel we go right out the door and it's just like water off a duck's back. We're not doing anything. I don't know how to put it in words, but somehow we've got to get on fire for the Lord. There's got to be a change in each one of us, including myself.

How does that happen? Have you got any ideas?

I think each one of us should spend more time with the Lord. My best time is very early in the morning. I try to get up between five o'clock and 5:30 in the morning, unless I sleep late and get up around six o'clock, but I still try to take an hour in the morning for reading my Sabbath School lesson and the Bible, and I pray. I am not a good reader, and sometimes I have to read over and over again to understand.

If each one of us, including myself, will just take the time, the Holy Spirit will teach us what we need to know. We need to take more time to be on our knees and just thank the Lord every day.

Sometimes we don't know why things occur the way they do. I've experienced that in my life. But many times I've looked back and felt that bad days have been a blessing. You see things happening, and you learn from those experiences. And I truly believe we need to spend more time on our knees, praying for others, and reading the Bible.

I think of a dear friend of mine who died this past week in Florida. I would call and talk to him a couple of times a week when he was there. His wife told me when she called me last week after he died, "All he thought about was church, heaven, and Jesus. Just a couple of nights before he died, he was praying and pouring out his heart for others and the church." Then she said, "I just went to sleep. I don't even know when he came to bed."

I thought of myself and felt I should be doing more of that. Praying for others.

I truly believe I changed as a result of that one brother's prayers. I also know my mom prayed and prayed. I think I am back in the church today because of the many who prayed for me, and because the Holy Spirit was drawing me back.

How important is your Lord to you today?

Very important. I wish I were a better reader than I am. I read so slow. But I know Jesus gave so much for me, and I am here today because of what He gave and did for me. He gave all. He's given His life for all. I love to read *The Desire of Ages* and learn about His life as a youngster and what He went through on the cross for me. I feel I am not worth it. God is so good to me I just want to praise His name.

Questions

1. When Adventists do business with those who have left the church, how should we relate to them? What is our responsibility to them? to the church? to God?

2. How can we encourage the workaholic to consider the results of such a lifestyle? How can we encourage a change in such behavior?

3. The Protestant work ethic is an accepted way of life for most Adventists. How can such people be helped when that lifestyle disrupts family life? when it takes people away from God and the church?

4. Is it possible that the workaholic who "repents" of long work days might transfer that energy to church work? If so, how has life changed for the person or his/her family? Is workaholism as much a danger to the Christian life as alcoholism? What is the difference between dedication and workaholism? Does the church have a responsibility to help workaholics change their lifestyle?

5. How can one develop a balance in church, home, and work activities to maintain a positive Christian lifestyle?

Conclusions

Pat Habada

The Call to Return

So some people decided to come back to church. So what?

We interviewed ten people hoping to gain some insights from their stories that would be of use to those who are serious about reclaiming former Adventists. What have we learned? Several things. Not the least of which is that the Holy Spirit is ready when we are. As long as we leave the door even slightly ajar, He doesn't give up on us. Even after twenty-five years, Ray still heard that Voice, reminding him that God wants to lead in his life, that he is still God's child, that God cares about him and his future. No matter how long one has been away, returning remains an option.

Early childhood influence

Eight out of the ten persons interviewed expressed memories of early childhood Adventism that reminded them of happy times in the church. Ray recalled pleas-

ant Sabbath School experiences. Lee Ann remembered
Pathfinder outings and kept in touch socially with the
people who directed those activities. John recalled family worships and Sabbath afternoons when the kids in
his family "played church." All these important memories drew these people back to God and His church.

Early childhood in Adventism is probably one of
the most significant factors in life that makes "coming back" possible. People remember, and they know
that the basic Adventist message is "right" or "true"
and that God will take them back.

Adventist education

What about Adventist education? Does it have an
influence on those who have turned away from God?
Consider the data. Three people never attended
Adventist schools. One, Ray, attended elementary
school for one year only but indicated that it was a
negative experience and he didn't want to talk about
it. Cherie attended for the seventh and eighth grades
only—her early teen years—and also indicated that
it was a negative experience. Lee Ann attended for
grades one through four and wanted to go to an
Adventist academy but was unable to do so. Bud received his first eight years of schooling in an Adventist
elementary school.

Jeff went to Adventist schools during his elementary and high school years and, although he made
many friends, indicated that his academy experience
was otherwise negative. Elizabeth graduated from an
Adventist academy and received the first two years
of her college education in an Adventist institution
before transferring to a public university. Tim attended Adventist schools all his life, through college,
later attending a public university. Although his "daily

existence was wrapped up in Adventism," church attendance "had no meaning," was "the biggest bother," and "was not the place where [he] was getting any answers."

Does all this tell us that the church needs to take a long look at the *real* impact of Adventist education? Certainly these interviews are not conclusive, and one should not draw from them that Adventist education leaves a negative influence in the lives of students. However, it does seem to indicate that more study should be given to imparting a lasting influence of such education on people both inside and out of the church.

Prayer

What role did prayer play in the return of these ten? Lee Ann, Cherie, Jeff, John, and Ray all indicated that the prayers of church friends and family members, particularly mothers, were important. Ray tells of church members who prayed for him throughout the twenty-five years he was away from God. Jeff talked about a non-Adventist friend who prayed for him. Cindy and Mike appreciated the prayers of church members during their time of uncertainty.

It is also interesting to note that when some of these people were "in the valley of decision" they went to their knees, seeking help from God. All of them recognize the importance of prayer life in maintaining their connection with God and the church. Is there ever a time when we should stop praying for others? We don't think so.

Marital concerns

Five of the subjects have been divorced and remarried. Two others experienced marital separations that lasted a year or more. Several of these people were married young, while still in their teens, to non-Adventists. Only one of those marriages has lasted. Jeff reports that his non-Adventist live-in girlfriend had an important influence on his decision to turn his life around. Their subsequent marriage and baptism have been an important part of their bonding with the church.

Can we draw any conclusions here? Although more study is needed, it seems apparent that these are factors that led some away from the church. Divorce among Adventists is no longer uncommon, and getting through the experience could and probably should be aided by the church through some kind of assistance such as counseling or divorce recovery groups. At the very least, church members need to be educated to accept the divorced without condemning or trying to place blame.

Personal contacts

Several of those interviewed told of contacts with Adventists during their time away from church. Ray said he sold produce to Adventists who came to his place of business. Those customers were friendly, but he didn't recall any invitations to return to church or any talks about his connection with Adventism. Tim was in touch with Adventists throughout his time away from church, but few of them knew what he was experiencing—and that was the way he wanted it. Cindy and Mike often found themselves caught in the middle of unpleasant controversy surrounding offshoot movements. Elizabeth's contacts were clouded by her experience with an abusive husband. Still, the loaf of bread delivered by a friendly member had an impact she remembers. Lee Ann recalled social contacts with former Pathfinder leaders. Most of the contacts with "Adventists in good and regular standing" were with one's parents, and some of them were negative. Jeff recalled moving out of his parents' home because he couldn't get along with them.

Five people reported pastoral visits. Jeff talked about "a couple of visits" from pastors but indicated that nothing good came of them and expressed his opinion that they were negative as far as he was concerned. Cherie described her visit with a pastor in which he said, "We want you back," and she responded, "No way am I coming back to this church." She indicated that he seemed to be condescending, although she did recognize that her own attitude probably had something to do with his response to her. Lee Ann reported that the pastor came to discuss removing her name from the church records, not to encourage her to come back to church.

John had perhaps the most rewarding pastoral visit, since he and the pastor became lasting friends and keep in contact even though that pastor has moved to another part of the country.

Is it possible that pastors need some guidance in how to approach those who have left the church? Obviously, most people in that category have no interest in pastoral visits; they usually want to be left alone. The last person they want to see is an Adventist pastor—until they are considering returning to the church. How does a pastor or church member know how to initiate conversations during these times? Is it possible to become too persistent—as Gary was in his contacts with Cherie, contacts that eventually led her to agree to go to church for just one Sabbath?

The right reason?

It would appear that some people came back to church—not back to God. And there is a difference. Some expressed a desire to straighten out their lives—

to get rid of unhealthy lifestyles. Others were afraid they would be "lost" or that probation would close and they would be left out. Others identified the influence of the Holy Spirit in telling them they were living sinful lives and decided to live by the rules they had been taught as children. In some cases these were the drawing cards, the beginnings that led to a new relationship with God. Others still seem to be stuck in a kind of legalism that says "If I am good, God will save me—from myself, from my lifestyle, from things that will harm me."

In several cases, subjects acknowledged that a lasting relationship is built on communication with God through daily Bible study and prayer, which is sometimes put aside because of pressing concerns of family and work responsibilities. In two instances, the birth of children and concern for their upbringing led mothers back to church.

Again, it would be helpful to look more carefully at reasons and where they lead as people make decisions to return to the church.

Personal attitude

True, some were dragged back, kicking and screaming, as they confronted marital problems, bad habits, offshoot movements, and the will to change. Both Jeff and Ray struggled with God. Jeff "wrestled" all night before making his move. Ray bargained, "—If my wife will take me back I will—" Cherie went to church only because she wanted to be rid of a pesky Adventist. Tim thought he should maintain a semblance of spirituality and managed to do so—something not entirely uncommon among many church members today. Cindy and Mike had to move from being critical and judgmental to become accepting of and be accepted by others. John had to lay aside perceptions of feeling unloved by church members.

Is it worth it?

The attitudes and the reasons may not have been the best, but each one made a decision to return, to change, to try again, to submit to God's will. Therein lies the core, the determination to do what they believe to be right. And that is just the beginning. Out of that determination can come valuable growth toward God and His kingdom of love and understanding.

The reception

To love, or not to love. To encourage, neglect, or ignore. These are the questions to ask of church members. John found himself in a largely unloving church community. Fortunately, he didn't let this keep him away. He determined he would return to God regardless of the attitude of church members. In most other cases, church members received the returning "like the prodigal son," as Lee Ann put it. Open hearts, open arms, and open doors project positive images to those who are struggling both within and without the church.

Activities such as baby and wedding showers evoke pleasant feelings of acceptance and caring. Invitations to participate in social gatherings, Bible study groups, and youth groups make positive impressions. Those who are returning want to become involved. Jeff expressed that desire when he said he would "maybe become a deacon." Tim got involved in the Salt company, a meaningful experience for him.

Should we throw caution to the winds? Probably not. Perhaps there are times when we want to be sure about intentions and goals. But it is possible to be accepting, even if we aren't sure about a person's future.

Christ ate with sinners—so can we. People may come back to church for the wrong reasons, but it is a beginning. Often whether they stay and grow is up to us, to the way we respond to their presence, to the gifts they bring to the church family, and yes, to their troubles and woes. "Inasmuch as ye have done it unto one of the least of these" is still worth thinking about.